Patience&
Perfection

FINDING PEACE IN GOD'S PLAN FOR YOU!

Daniel E. Paavola

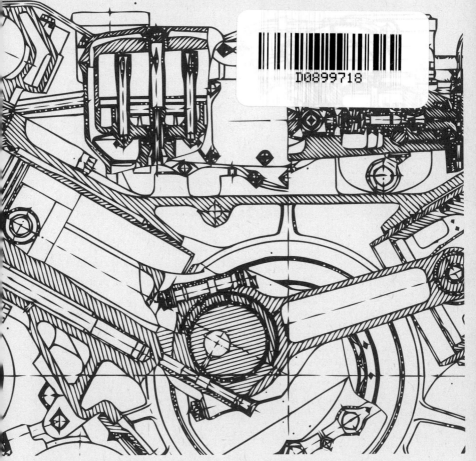

D0899718

CONCORDIA PUBLISHING HOUSE · SAINT LOUIS

Concordia
Publishing House

Published by Concordia Publishing House
3558 S. Jefferson Avenue, St. Louis, MO 63118–3968
1-800-325-3040 • cph.org

Manufactured in the United States of America

LIBRARY OF CONGRESS CATALOGING-IN-PUBLICATION DATA

Library of Congress Cataloging-in-Publication Data
Names: Paavola, Daniel E., author.
Title: Patience and perfection : finding peace in God's plan for you / Daniel Paavola.
Description: St. Louis : Concordia Publishing House, 2018.
Identifiers: LCCN 2018029926 (print) | LCCN 2018031516 (ebook) | ISBN 9780758660138 | ISBN 9780758660077
Subjects: LCSH: Perfection--Religious aspects--Christianity. | Patience--Religious aspects--Christianity. | Bible--Criticism, interpretation, etc. | Perfection--Biblical teaching. | Patience--Biblical teaching.
Classification: LCC BT766 (ebook) | LCC BT766 .P23 2018 (print) | DDC 231.7--dc23
LC record available at https://lccn.loc.gov/2018029926

1 2 3 4 5 6 7 8 9 10   27 26 25 24 23 22 21 20 19 18

CONTENTS

ACKNOWLEDGMENTS

Bacon and eggs. Coffee and doughnuts. A good book and a comfortable chair. Some things just go together. Each is fine by itself, but who wants a doughnut with no coffee? We want the whole package.

Perfection and patience. Are you seeing these two as a natural pair, the spiritual match to the chair and book? Maybe not. Either one is fine, but together perfection and patience could cancel each other out. We want perfection, at least from God, and we can make a good case that perfection is what He should deliver. After all, He is perfect, and the world He made began that way. But if perfection is too much to ask, then I suppose we can settle for patience. But isn't asking for patience just admitting that perfection will never come?

In this book, we'll find a union of patience and perfection that might surprise us. We'll study seven biblical themes that are repeated actions combining God's perfection and patience. Patience is the essence of God's walk with us, and His perfection draws us to Himself each day. Though we'll never keep to a perfect line, He persists in walking with us. His patience is His perfect, strong hold on us.

This interplay of patience and perfection in the seven themes comes from my patient students who have developed these themes with me over the years of teaching at Concordia University Wisconsin. Thank you to everyone who has shared class with me and has provided many of the examples here. Thank you also to my colleagues at Concordia who have studied these repeated biblical ideas with me. In particular, my friends in the school of nursing were wonderful in shaping chapter 8, and Dr. James Freese gave excellent ideas on the choice of hymns as examples of the seven themes.

Besides the many at Concordia University, thanks go to the editors and others at Concordia Publishing House for their creative work on this project. Special thanks go to Laura Lane, my editor. Her encouragement made each day of writing more hopeful, and her editing made each page much better. Finally, thanks goes to my family for their patience with this project during very busy family times. My wife, Holly, and our three children, Christy, Steve, and Nicole, are wonderful examples of biblical patience and perfect love and care.

Blessings to you as you follow these themes and see how divine patience and perfection intertwine in our lives.

CHAPTER 1

PERFECT? REALLY?

You have to buy new clothes. You've put it off as long as you can, but now there's no escape. The clothes are not the problem. It's the dressing room, that little place with unfocused mirrors and a pincushion's worth of discarded pins. You really don't want to go there, but you have to. Taylor, who loves you, has come shopping with you, and Taylor insists that this time you are actually going to try these clothes on.

Taylor chooses a whole new outfit for you: shirt, pants, belt, even socks and shoes. Taylor puts them into your arms, points you to the dressing room, and says, "Go. I'll wait here." That's code for "Put these on and come out here wearing them." This time there'll be no carrying the clothes out and promising, "They fit fine." This time, Taylor wants proof.

It's the mirrors, the pins, and the stiffness of it all that gets you. The mirrors in the dressing room are on three sides, showing you a profile you didn't know you had. It's shocking to see what others look at every day. Maybe that's why people are always smiling at you. The pins are everywhere in these clothes, and when you've taken twelve of them out of the shirt, there's one more waiting in the collar, aimed at your artery. And then there's the stiffness of it all. The shoes have a knife edge around the top, the belt won't bend around your waist, and the holes for the shirt buttons act like they're still sewn shut.

But eventually you have it all on. You have to go out now. Stay any longer and Taylor is going to come to the dressing room door and ask, "Are you okay in there?" To prevent that, you open the door and step out.

Taylor is not alone. There's a semicircle of people waiting for their loved one to come out. The sound of the dressing room door opening gave them all hope, so they all watch as you step out. Everyone looks you over, even though they know in an instant you're not the one they want to see. They take in the shirt, hastily tucked, the belt straining to go around, the pants with one cuff tucked into a shoe. They all smile. It's a smile that says, "Are you sure about this?"

You're not sure. That's the point. You know this isn't working, and you are a half step from turning around and going back. But then Taylor takes one step forward, looks you over again, actually smiles, and says, "Perfect." It's so loud and so surprising that everyone else looks you over again. But they only smile one more time and then stare at Taylor with a look that says, "Really? You think so?"

You've got an answer. "I don't think I've got all this on right. I know I missed a button somehow, and something didn't line up right. And there's still a pin in here somewhere. These shoes are really tight, and I think I'm standing funny in them." Taylor hears all this, but it doesn't seem to register. Taking one step closer to you, Taylor says it again, "Perfect."

Now that you two are a little closer, you dare to say, "Well, if I got back on the diet and actually lost those ten pounds, then maybe this would work better." You're also ready to suggest that going to the gym wouldn't hurt and that it's also one terrible hair day. But you don't get to say that. By now, Taylor is right in front of you, puts a finger on your lips, stops your mumbling, and says for the third time, "Perfect."

> Taking one step closer to you, Taylor says it again, "Perfect."

And you are, if Taylor says you are. At that point, you have to decide who to believe. Do you trust the mirrors in the dressing room and the people standing outside? Or do you trust Taylor, who said only the same word three times, but said it as though it were true? I say, trust Taylor. You're perfect.

That's the surprising judgment of God over us. Hebrews 10:14 says, "For by a single offering He has perfected for all time those who are being sanctified." The single sacrifice of Jesus is the basis for the judgment of God over us. In that judgment, God declares us perfect in His sight. It is not a perfection of our promises or progress. It is the perfection of His choice, His sight over us.

In this book, we'll study the perfection that comes from God. When we seek perfection from and with God, remember that it is a perfection of His sight and His judgment. It might be a perfection hidden from the rest of the world and, at times, hidden also from us. But God's perfection joins with His distinctive patience to announce that which Taylor said, "Perfect."

To hear and believe this is much like the story of the dressing room. For example, when we worship, we go through the dressing room experience. We enter with our old clothes, stained with the knowledge of our sins. We put on the new clothes of forgiveness, and in fact, we are clothed in Baptism with Christ Himself (Galatians 3:27). However, when we step out of worship into the familiar circle of those who know us, we wonder, "Is this really true?" Those who see us don't see perfection. They have that same indulgent smile, at best, that asks, "Perfect? Really? You think so?" And we would all be quick to offer up the same excuses we've used for years. You're not perfect, but you're trying. If work wasn't so busy right now, if Mom didn't make you so angry every time you talked, if all the bills didn't come all at once, you'd be better.

To all that, God takes a step closer and says, "Perfect." Again, you don't see anything close to perfection, but you might suggest to God that, given a little more time, you could be better. Maybe if you started getting up earlier and had a more peaceful start to the day, did some thinking and praying. Maybe if you didn't watch the news so much and get so upset by everything that's happening.

Maybe . . .

In the midst of the maybes, God steps right up to you, puts His finger on your lips, and stops your mumbling, excusing, and promising. He looks deeply into your eyes and says, "Perfect." He's not talking to someone else, and He's not talking about a someday you won't likely ever see. He's talking about you, now, and it's true.

PERFECTION IS MARRIED TO PATIENCE

God's declaration of "Perfect" is true, but it takes time for us to take it all in. That's the role of patience, one of the great spiritual gifts. But patience is not only a gift for us to exercise. Patience is the quality perhaps most married to God's perfection. God's view of us as perfect includes His divine patience. He declares us innocent as a timeless, eternal truth. "There is therefore now no condemnation for those who are in Christ Jesus" (Romans 8:1). This perfection is our present reality and is the partner with God's patience over us. God's patience is built upon His declaration that we are perfect in His sight, a sight that doesn't change. Because of that judgment, God has all patience with us.

> God steps right up to you, puts His finger on your lips, and stops your mumbling, excusing, and promising.

Patience can only last where God's perfect judgment is already in place. Imagine if we were not already justified in our relationship with God. Then what patience with God might we find? If we were not declared to be justified by Christ's sacrifice and resurrection, if we were not declared to be innocent and even perfect in God's sight, how long would His patience last? Patience looks for progress. Patience wants promises kept. Patience needs a purpose for all its waiting. But despite our best intentions, we find ourselves faltering in a Romans 7 frustration. The good that we would do, we don't, and the evil that we would end, we continue in it. Left to that failure, we can only wonder when God's patience will end. We would have to conclude with Paul in Romans 7:24 "Wretched man that I am!" God's patience should end with a thunderclap, a lightning bolt, and His words of agreement, "Yes, you are wretched!"

But God's patience is founded on the perfection that has already come in His Son. At Jesus' Baptism and His transfiguration, the Father says, "This is My beloved Son, with whom I am well pleased" (Matthew 3:17; 17:5). God doesn't wait anxiously for a dimly reflected, quickly passing perfection that we might offer Him. He doesn't snatch a moment of perfect reflection, a spiritual firefly that glows only long enough to be noticed but never long enough to be kept. God has seen perfection on earth already in Christ. He has seen that perfection in His Son for eternity and displayed that perfection throughout His years on earth. Now God has extended that perfection to us. He sees all those in Christ in a marriage relationship with His Son—He as the true, ideal Husband and we believers as the perfect Bride. Paul describes God's view of us in that marriage relationship with Christ, who has "cleansed her by the washing of the water with the word, so that He might present the church to Himself in splendor, without spot or wrinkle or any such thing, that she might be holy and without blemish" (Ephesians 5:26–27). This view of absolute perfection brings patience. In fact, perfection and patience make up the wedding party, the maid of honor and the best man.

> Patience can only last where God's perfect judgment is already in place.

Weddings take ages to plan, and they prove that by never starting on time. Weddings need patience. It is often not the fault of the bride but someone else like the photographer who shows up an hour late. The groom is left waiting and wondering what's taking so long. A wise groom just waits and says, "No problem. She'll be perfect." Only a fool greets his bride at the altar by saying,

"You're late." A wise groom greets her, no matter what the time is, and says, "You're perfect." She is exactly the vision he has always had. It's not that he could only now see her like this, dressed without blemish or imperfection. He's always seen her this way. That's what happens when patience and perfection come together. When these two are at the center, that's a marriage that lasts.

God creates that union between Himself and us. He supplies both the perfection in His view of us and the patience by which He waits and walks with us. We learn at least a measure of His patience and trust upon His perfect plan and will. We begin to adapt our expectations to Psalm 46:10: "Be still, and know that I am God." Knowing the perfection of God's power and mercy, we can say with David in Psalm 27:13–14, "I believe that I shall look upon the goodness of the LORD in the land of the living! Wait for the LORD; be strong, and let your heart take courage; wait for the LORD!" While we haven't seen yet all that God plans to do with and for us, the sharing of His patience with us must be one of the most important steps He has in mind for us.

> He supplies both the perfection in His view of us and the patience by which He waits and walks with us.

This combination of patience and perfection is the foundation of this book and the seven biblical themes we're going to discuss. The repeated actions of God in the Bible show an interplay between these two. Patience and perfection need each other to be fulfilled. Taken separately, they would stand out in any list of what we expect of God. We might even put them at the top of our list of what defines God for us. He is perfect, of course, and He is patient toward us. However, we're speaking of more than qualities on a list. We want to see how these two interplay throughout our understanding of God and our relationship with Him. To do that, our understanding of God's perfection has to be broadened a bit. We likely want an instant perfection, but greater patience might be needed in our understanding of God.

Our Perfection Is Brittle

It was perfect. Just look at it. Get closer if you want, but don't touch it! Your fingerprints would be the first thing wrong with it. Just look at it. You don't need to inspect it because there's nothing wrong with it. Just take it all in. From every angle, see what you knew you would see. Perfection.

I hope you've had this experience. Was it your first new car? Maybe it was the diamond engagement ring, still in the box. It was your first home, the house you actually were buying, not just renting. One way or another, I hope you've seen perfection at first sight.

Of course, perfection is a brittle thing. It's waiting to break at our first touch. Even looking too hard might be too harsh. Looking too hard might invite us to imagine some imperfection that we never noticed before. Perfection is a sharp point, a single moment that neither waits nor lasts. And so, given just a bit of time, that new car became the old, dented thing you sold for less than what was your single monthly payment. After a year, the house needed new gutters, a new roof, a new garage door, and a new furnace. It still looks good as you drive to it, but you're wondering if it wouldn't look even better if you were driving away from it.

Wouldn't it be wonderful if perfection both existed and lasted? What if new cars stayed new, right down to that wonderful smell? What if new houses always had clean walls and new carpets with no worn paths? And let's have engagement rings always express not just the hope but also the reality of a perfect relationship. We'd all agree: let perfection come, and let it last.

Wouldn't God be for this, our desire for perfection? After all, God is the ultimate in perfection Himself. He has no error, no fault, no weakening or stopping. Isaiah 40:28 says, "Have you not known? Have you not heard? The LORD is the everlasting God, the Creator of the ends of the earth. He does not faint or grow weary; His understanding is unsearchable." God's perfection was expressed in Genesis 1 and 2 through His creation, and His own judgment on all He made was "It is good." We have every reason to expect that God will bring about perfection as a central quality by which we know Him. Further, wouldn't it be reasonable for God to protect that perfection when it comes? We can't lock up a car in a sealed garage or safeguard every carpet in our home, but couldn't God keep His world just as He wants?

> Perfection is a sharp point, a single moment that neither waits nor lasts.

PERFECTION COMES IN PIECES

However, this expectation has several problems. First, how do we know what perfection is? What we judge perfect is limited by the little we know. We're far from Eden, so our experience with perfection is a worn hand-me-down. In this area especially, we are children, as Paul said. "For we know in part and we prophecy in part, but when the perfect comes, the partial will pass away" (1 Corinthians 13:9–10). Perhaps we need a wider view of what might be called perfect.

I know a man, Brady, who restores motorcycles to like-new condition at his shop, Retrospeed in Belgium, Wisconsin. When he's done, the bike is at least as good as it was when it left the Honda, Ducati, or Suzuki factory fifty years ago. His bikes are masterpieces that are on the cover of national magazines, and they sell for deservedly high prices. With even a glance at one of his bikes, you would say, "Perfect."

But that's not how he finds these bikes. For example, when a 1977 Ducati 900 SuperSport came into his shop, it was in terrible shape. Engine dead, tires flat, chrome scratched, chain rusted solid. In other words, it was perfect. Perfect because it came in pieces. Perfect because it gave Brady something to work on and perfect because, while it was found in a field in Texas, it was finally in Wisconsin, ready to be worked on. Perfect because it showed Brady's talents. When you hear the story of the restoration, you want to see what Brady started with just as much as you want to see the completed bike. You need the "before" pictures to appreciate the "after" pictures.

Perhaps we don't recognize God's perfection because we want only the "after" pictures. We want to be the "after" picture of perfection. We imagine that we could embody perfection now if God would only set His hand to the task; we imagine that He should and could keep us in that perfect state. However, our sad experience living east of Eden is that we are always in motion, either motion toward God's perfection or away from it. In this life, with the burden of original sin, we cannot achieve any lasting state of perfect living. We're declared justified by God's grace and are seen as innocent by God's choice through the sacrifice of His Son. But our actual experience feels far from that, so we end up echoing Paul in Romans 7:18–19: "For I have the desire to do what is right, but not the ability to carry it out. For I do not do the good I want, but the evil I do not want is what I keep on doing."

Any perfection we might have is not in the place we are now. Our present location is not perfection. Tomorrow's destination won't be perfection. Only our direction might be our perfection.

We want to be the "after" picture of perfection. Since we're in motion, our sole hope is that we are in the direction of God's plan. Paul again speaks of this in Philippians 3:12–14: "Not that I have already obtained this or am already perfect, but I press on to make it my own, because Christ Jesus has made me His own. Brothers, I do not consider that I have made it my own. But one thing I do: forgetting what lies behind and straining forward to what lies ahead, I press on toward the goal for the prize of the upward call of God in Christ Jesus." Our restoration process is long, much like Brady working on a forty-year-old Ducati. If there are pieces strewn about and things seem more apart than together, remember, you should have seen how it looked when it came in. So we also are declared perfect by God even in the middle of a long restoration, far from any visible perfection.

That restoration is a daily journey. Our direction, however small and faltering, comes under that grace of God and is even found acceptable to Him purely by grace. Every parent who has taught a daughter or son to drive knows this use of "perfect" in regard to motion and direction. You take your daughter out to drive, or even better, to practice parallel parking. It won't be fast or pretty. But you'll say "Great" and "Perfect" a lot. As long as the wheel is turned roughly in the right direction, the transmission is in reverse or drive as it should be, and her foot is on either the brake or throttle, but not both at the same time, it's "Perfect." You might still end up a foot from the curb with the left front fender sticking out a little in the traffic lane, but "Honey, it's perfect."

So God is in motion with us. Our vision of perfection might be a spotless Lexus parallel parked on the street, three inches from the curb. But God understands that we're a hand-me-down Honda with one wheel, at best, a foot from the curb. But in Christ, God declares us perfect. Again Paul speaks of this at the end of his discussion on the thorn in the flesh and his request that God remove it. God's answer helps Paul recognize this perfection in imperfection: "But He said to me, 'My grace is sufficient for you, for My power is made perfect in weakness.' Therefore I will boast all the more gladly of my weaknesses, so that the power of Christ may rest upon me" (2 Corinthians 12:9). Our perfection is in God's proclamation that we are not guilty; His proclamation is complete and perfect by the work of Christ. We see this perfection in action in how God patiently walks with us in our weakness and demonstrates His power through our faltering steps.

> In Christ, God declares us perfect.

God's Method of Perfection

So one of the challenges we have is seeing God declare an active perfection over our imperfect motion. We see perfection by God's declaration of mercy, not by any state we have achieved. But another challenge of God's unique perfection is recognizing the means He uses to express this mercy. We can understand that we might not be perfect, but certainly we can expect God to be. Yet when we see His mercy in action, it looks far from perfect.

Of course, God is perfect by any standard of holiness. Isaiah's breathtaking view of God announces this with the cries of the seraphim: "Holy, holy, holy is the LORD of hosts; the whole earth is full of His glory" (Isaiah 6:3). But Isaiah is also afraid of God's holiness because he is a man of unclean lips, living among equally sinful people: "Woe is me! . . . For my eyes have seen the King, the LORD of hosts!" (Isaiah 6:5). Given such a view as this, our awe and fear of God's perfection would be just as immediate and obvious.

We can see this expression of God's perfection repeatedly in the Old and New Testaments. One of the biblical themes in this book, "What Does Greatness Look Like?" expresses this expectation. The transfiguration of Jesus might be the highpoint of this visible and convincing perfection. Jesus shines like the sun while the Father speaks from the clouds. The sight and sound of such perfect glory reduce the disciples to an Isaiah-like fear coupled with a desire to see more. God's perfection draws us close enough to watch but distant enough to escape.

However, God has chosen a different method of perfection through the ministry and especially the death of Jesus. His perfection is that of the servant, the One who emptied Himself and became obedient to death, even death on the cross, as Paul summarizes in Philippians 2:6–8. He is the One who chose on the cross to be despised: "He had no form or majesty that we should look at Him, and no beauty that we should desire Him. He was

despised and rejected by men, a man of sorrows and acquaint-
ed with grief" (Isaiah 53:2–3). Perfection came as He steadfastly
looked upon our sin, carried our sin away,
and healed us by His wounds. How strange **When we see**
is this perfection? We cannot bear to see **His mercy in**
His perfection on the cross, but He can **action, it looks**
bear to see all our sins. Christ, the holy Son
of God, was transformed in His bearing of **far from perfect.**
our sin. "For our sake He made Him to be-
come sin who knew no sin, so that in Him we might become the
righteousness of God" (2 Corinthians 5:21).

We don't expect this change as the path to perfection. Brady
transforms the broken pieces into a whole, perfect motorcycle.
He takes it apart, but he doesn't destroy it. If a gas tank has original, perfect paint, he keeps it. If the original pistons have perfect
compression, he doesn't burn a hole through them. But God, in
restoring us, afflicts all that which is imperfect onto His Son even
to the point of death and says at His broken death on Good Friday,
"Perfect."

That perfect bearing of sin is the companion to God's patience. God not only sees us as the spotless Bride, but He also has
seen the complete destruction of our sin through His Son. His
anger is not building up with an impatient boiling, eager to pour
over us. He has put that anger into the death of His Son so that a
new patience exists between Himself and us.

THE SEVEN THEMES UNITE
PATIENCE AND PERFECTION

The seven biblical themes that we explore in this book develop
this union of patience and perfection. Of course, there are aspects
of both qualities that are expected and others that are a surprise.
A brief overview of the seven themes can help us think about
God's patience, which fulfills our expectation for His perfection.

The first theme takes these two qualities on directly: "Instant Perfection—Patient Relationship." In this theme, we explore God's perfection through His actions throughout the Bible. From the creation in Genesis 1 and 2 through the perfection we see and yearn for in Revelation, we find God creating and restoring His world. We see perfection in the life and work of His Son, especially in His instant actions of healing that make the lame walk, the deaf hear, and the dead man step forth.

But as much as we yearn for this perfection, God offers another dimension in His tie with us—patient relationship. While perfection could come in a greater measure in our lives, God answers our impatience with His perfect patience in relationship. He helps us realize that our walk together is worth as much or more than the destination. The true wonder is not that God is perfect, but that He wants to be in a patient relationship with us. Together, these two dimensions of one theme give us God's essential qualities, patience and perfection.

The dual nature of the first theme leads to the second theme, "It's Not the First, but the Second That Counts." Both the nature of Hebraic repetition and God's actions in Genesis show this love of the second over the first. God's enduring relationship with a fallen world isn't merely playing out a losing hand; God's relationship with the world shows His creativity and plan. Frequently, it appears that the second is preferred over the first in the Bible. Jacob is blessed over his brother Esau, and David, the second king, is greater than Saul. Jesus comes as the Second Adam, far beyond the first. Patience is needed as we step from the first to the greater second.

This emphasis on the second points to the third theme: "One Stands in Place of Us All." At first, this principle rankles us. Why should we bear the punishment of another's failure? But when the Second Adam succeeds in our place and His triumph becomes ours, then this is a wonderful principle. Goliath was right when he challenged the army of Israel to send a champion against him;

we don't all need to fight, but we can let one stand in our place. Then the victories of David and the greater victories of David's Son come to us all. Perfection will come with His work, but it takes patience to wait as He steps forward in our place.

This is pure good news, but what an effect it has for us. God is with us. Surely life will be better, starting now. But the fourth theme, "Grace Upends Our World," reminds us that the gracious presence of God still leads us into the path of danger and difficulty. The people of Israel, even after God sends Moses to free them, must make bricks without straw. Mary hears the wonderful news that the Messiah will be born of her, but she also hears that Joseph plans to divorce her. Paul is met by Jesus on the road, yet he's blind for three days. Grace upends our world, but it does so through difficulties we never imagined.

This combination of good news and difficulty captures the two sides of the fifth theme, "What Does Greatness Look Like?" This is a principle taken from Bruce Catton's history of General U. S. Grant, *Grant Moves South*. We expect that power and glory ought to look like power and glory. Shouldn't a general wear a spotless uniform and be mounted on a magnificent horse? Biblically, we see this version of greatness when Solomon's wisdom dazzles all and the temple reflects the glory of God. But glory can also look strange and hidden. Grant was known to go about camp in a mud-stained private's coat with no insignia at all. And so David, though anointed as king, lived in caves while being hunted by Saul, and his greatness was in sparing Saul's life. Jesus' miracles came with both measures of greatness. He showed the obvious glory of the transfiguration but also showed the hidden glory of One who saved others but would not save Himself from the cross.

That willingness to die is the heart of the sixth theme, "God Cures with the Illness Itself." We cure with the opposite of illness.

> Grace upends our world, but it does so through difficulties we never imagined.

We cure hunger with food, fatigue with rest, and cold with a warm blanket. And we want to make this exchange in an instant. But God surprises us by choosing the illness itself as the cure, though that cure might not come immediately. God cured those bitten by snakes in the exodus by giving them a bronze snake to look upon. God cured death by placing His Son into a body of death, ending sin by being made sin Himself. He grasps the illness to Himself, giving healing to us.

But waiting for this cure can leave us in a dark place. Then we need the assurance of the final theme, "Perfection Welcomes Failure." Of course, this is not how our world usually works. Perfection frightens failure. But God draws all men to Himself through the perfect life and death of Jesus. Hebrews 4 reminds us that though He was tempted in all things as we are, He never failed. And therefore, we draw near to His throne of grace. Frightened Peter dared to step out of the boat when he saw the perfectly powerful Jesus walk on the waves. The perfect Gospel not only lets us come but also draws us out of our fear. In the end, the Bible concludes with the perfection of a new heaven and a new earth, an absolute perfection that welcomes us home.

A Balance of Expectation and Surprise

These seven themes express then the tension between perfection and patience. In doing this, they have another tension: expectation and surprise. These themes are patterns of God's action that we can see repeatedly throughout Scripture. The themes are significant enough that we anticipate them happening again and again. But when are they going to come? That is the question, and we might be surprised where we see these themes. We might be surprised when we find a new expression of God's perfection in the most unlikely place.

These seven themes not only keep us wondering when each is going to reappear. These themes also unite the whole Bible under seven patterns. As we see the patterns appear over and over again, we might feel a natural familiarity combined with a desire for something more. Hebrews 1:1–2 expresses this in a broad way by saying, "Long ago, at many times and in many ways, God **The perfect Gospel not only lets us come but also draws us out of our fear.** spoke to our fathers by the prophets, but in these last days He has spoken to us by His Son." The continuity of the message from prophets to Son is clear, just as there is also the expectation that the Son will bring a new dimension to this revelation.

So, as the seven themes unfold throughout the Bible, we welcome their repetition. For example, the theme "One Stands in Place of Us All" is easily seen through the kings, prophets, and priests of the Old Testament. Yet we know that the ultimate One in place of us all comes only in the Son of God. We're intrigued to see God repeatedly choose and bless the second over the first through the Old Testament, but we know that the full use of that theme will be in Jesus, the new Adam.

Throughout this book, we'll see how the seven themes lead to Jesus but also how the themes intertwine. Our last chapter will highlight this, and you'll anticipate that as you see examples of each individual theme. David, the shepherd boy who dares to step out against Goliath, is both an example of one person standing in place of us all and also an example of greatness looking like greatness in the most surprising way. Not only do the themes intertwine, but they also lead you to expand them or develop new repeated patterns for yourself. Read with this tension between your expectations of these themes versus the surprise of where you find them. It's all like a trip down a north woods river.

Our Trip down the River

The Chippewa River of northern Wisconsin is perfect for canoeing with a seven-year-old boy. In the deep woods west of the small town of Glidden, the Chippewa meanders through the Chequamegon National Forest. The river is only two or three feet deep, usually fifty or so feet wide, going no faster than a man can walk. There are a few rocks but no raging rapids. On the banks is the unbroken northern forest.

Our family went canoeing on the Chippewa River for years, but usually it was a trip for our son, Steve, and me. We would drive about a half hour from our home in Butternut into the Chequamegon Forest to a canoe landing. Unload the canoe, get the life vests and paddles out, and push the canoe into the river. Let's go canoeing!

Now imagine that our son didn't want to go. By the way, Steve was always ready to go camping or canoeing, but for this story let's imagine he's afraid of getting into the canoe. If I ask him why, he'll say, "I don't know what's around the bend." The Chippewa is constantly turning, so you never see more than about fifty yards at a time. Steve's worried that something terrible is waiting around the bend. He's seen too many Disney videos where unsuspecting people come around a river bend to find a hundred-foot waterfall. So he's worried that around this bend, the Chippewa is going to plunge us to our death.

What do you say? You could start with "Steve, this isn't a cartoon." Then explain that the river we see here is the river we will have around the bend. How deep will it be? The same: two or three feet. How fast will it go? Just like here. We can walk faster. What's on the banks? Trees, trees, and trees.

That should do it. The river we have here is the river we'll have around the bend. If it weren't, we would never dare to go canoeing. Real rivers are generally the same from bend to bend, or they let you know by their roaring that something is coming. But generally, the river you have here is the river that is coming.

Now, if this were a movie, Steve should say, "Great, Dad, let's go!" But what if he does this: he looks down the river as far as he can see, turns to look up the river, and then says, "Okay, Dad, let's go home."

What's he thinking now? Well, he's seen it all. If the river here is the same as around the bend, why go? Look up and down and you've got it. Let's go home—maybe he'll even help load the canoe.

No, we're not going home. You don't go on the river to see the same thing. You go to see what you've never seen, or what you saw just that one time and maybe you'll see again. What's around the river bend? Maybe this time it will be a whitetail deer and her fawn drinking from the river. (Be quiet, Steve, and don't slap that blue plastic paddle of yours against the canoe so much.) Maybe we'll see the king of the forest, the black bear. Or best of all, we'll see a bald eagle in his nest or soaring above the river.

The deer, the bear, and the eagle don't line up at the boat landing to meet you. Even if you paddle under the eagle's nest, the eagle might not be there today. But that's the reason you have to go. The eagle might be there, or he might be fishing around the next bend. We won't know until we go. So get in the canoe. We're going around the river bend. (By the way, I'm writing this while sitting on the bank of another Wisconsin river on a perfect June day, looking at the river as it sweeps past me around a bend a hundred yards away. Perhaps I should stop writing, get in a canoe, and see what's around that bend today.)

THE BIBLE IS A CONTEXTUAL RIVER

Reading the Bible is like taking a river trip. The headwaters are Genesis 1, and from there, the river flows through almost countless turns. Each short narrative of a few verses is the hundred-yard-long stretch that you can see at this time. But we read by remembering where we've been. And we read by wondering what's going to come next. Come to the end of a particular story, finish a chapter, or reach the end of a person's life story, and you're ready to go around the bend.

Just like the Chippewa River, the Bible is both comfortingly familiar and also surprisingly new. We need consistency. The God we meet in Genesis 1 creates the world in great detail with approving love. Don't we want to meet that same God around every bend? The wonderful healer Jesus who just cleansed a leper or cast out a demon, don't we want to read next that He raised the dead son for his widowed mother? We dare not find a God who casts off the world as hopeless and hated. We won't keep reading if the healing Jesus next becomes a carpenter who kills His enemies with a single blow.

We read the Bible because of the consistent message it gives. We dare to move from the past of Genesis finally to the future of Revelation because of this consistency. In our use of the seven biblical themes, this is the consistency that makes these actions reliable themes. They can be counted on appearing around the bend. But they won't come on demand or with any numerical predictability. They come with the simple assurance that anything this important and striking will happen more than once. There's more than one bear, deer, and eagle in the forest. When you've seen one, you can plan on seeing another.

> Just like the Chippewa River, the Bible is both comfortingly familiar and also surprisingly new.

THREADS TO TIE IT ALL TOGETHER

As we go down the contextual river, we want to see connections between the seven themes as they appear. Each chapter will feature two unique sidebars. The pattern of these sidebars will highlight the connections in those themes. The first is the sense of a journey down a familiar road. We've all driven the same road over and over, only to be surprised at some point by something we notice for the first time. It's not that there's anything particularly new; you've just never noticed it before. So also the themes all use the biblical accounts that we know well. But now with the individual themes, there's something about them we've never seen before. Like we notice our neighbor's tree for the first time because it's in full bloom, so we also will see something new in the familiar Bible stories through these budding themes.

The other set of sidebars will feature a few wonderful hymns. These will likely be hymns that you know but have not thought of in terms of these seven themes. Like the houses and buildings we pass by every day without really seeing, perhaps we've sung these hymns without seeing their part in a larger biblical pattern. However, when all seven themes and hymns are done, then we have the complete picture that God has in mind.

Step Out of the Dressing Room

It's time to step out of the dressing room. We can't hide there. Despite our natural fears of appearing before God, we finally have to meet Him. But the wonderful news from these seven themes is that God meets us, says the first word Himself, and that word is "Perfect." In the coming seven themes, God repeats this message with a distinctive understanding of perfection that is married with patience. In the twisting river of biblical reading, we can both expect and be surprised by His repeated message. So turn the page, listen to Him, and hear Him say to you, "Perfect."

Discussion Questions

1. The opening story described reluctantly trying on new clothes. Is this something you also are reluctant to do? What would it mean for you to have someone greet you outside the dressing room and say to you, "Perfect"?

2. This chapter joined perfection and patience like a marriage. Why does each quality need the other (patience needs the ultimate goal of perfection, and only by patience will perfection be found)?

3. Define *perfection* quickly, perhaps with an image of what it would look like. It could start in any of these ways: "The perfect day would be . . ." "The perfect car would be . . ." "The perfect meal would have . . ." How is the life and work of Christ perfect in ways that we can see?

4. The seven biblical themes of the book were briefly explained. Which ones are the clearest to you now? Which ones leave you wondering what exactly is being described?

5. What value might there be in seeing biblical themes—
   that is, repeated actions, people, and places—that share
   a common message and yet are distinct each time they
   appear?

6. The canoe trip down the Chippewa River spoke of a
   combination of the familiar and the surprising. If not
   a canoe trip, what other activity gives you a similar
   combination of finding what you expect and yet being
   surprised?

7. If reading the Bible is like a canoe trip, how might that
   energize your Bible reading?

CHAPTER 2

INSTANT PERFECTION—
PATIENT RELATIONSHIP

The Model T Ford was a pile of tired, blue tin. The owner was the grandson of the man who had originally bought this car in 1917. Grandpa had brought it to this farm, and it had never left the farm or family. Imagine, essentially, a one-owner Model T! But don't get excited. It had been abandoned to a junk pile since 1953, left outside in northern Wisconsin with absolutely no protection. An open car with the top long gone, it had been buried under snow each winter for decades. It was sad, worn, and just wrong with its 1950's coat of blue house paint fading away.

But still, it was a Ford Model T. It still had the engine, transmission, and drivetrain intact. It had a hood and cowl and front fenders and four questionable wooden wheels. The engine turned over, but hadn't run since 1953. There was no top, no back seat, no rear fenders, and no rear doors. There was more missing than I wanted to admit. It was a cup just slightly more than half full, a sad little car that everyone had ignored.

But not this morning. My wife, Holly, and I stood in the farmer's yard near Ashland, Wisconsin, some fifty miles from our home in Butternut, Wisconsin. We had driven to see the car since the farmer had answered my ad in the local shopping paper. I was hoping to build a Model T from collected pieces. We couldn't afford a whole car, so I was beginning to build one from a frame here and a wheel there. Then the farmer answered the ad, offering his car, so we came to see.

The price? He wanted only $250 for a one-family-owned Model T still on the farm to which it was first delivered. Who gets a one-owner 1917 Model T for $250? I asked Holly if we should try to get it for $200. She said, "Just pay him the $250." Good advice. We paid, came back with a friend with a truck and trailer, and hauled it to our garage.

What were we thinking? There's more to the story than just an old car needing a home. The story begins in 1917 when both that Model T and my father were born. Dad was a farm boy in New York Mills, Minnesota, whose family's first car was a 1915 Ford Model T. Dad was a farmer for fifty years. When we bought the Model T, Dad was a year away from retiring from active farming. He and Mom would stay on the farm for several years, but we all wondered what Dad would do without farming. Dad was a natural-born mechanic, serving as a mechanic in the army during World War II. He loved welding and turning wrenches, but the hard, physical work of dairy farming was too much anymore. But what would Dad do, and what would Dad and I do together anymore? Being the only son, my relationship with Dad was our work together.

> It was a cup just slightly more than half full, a sad little car that everyone had ignored.

So I thought we should build a Model T. It would be like Dad's family's first car. Model Ts are simple and, since Ford made 15,000,000 of them, they're still common and about the cheapest old car there is. So we bought this beat-down 1917 from the Ashland farmer, and the adventure began.

Dad and I worked on that T for the next four years. We talked at least once a week on the phone. Dad and Mom came to visit, and Dad took parts home to work on. We went parts hunting together on below-zero days, pulling rusty parts out of snow banks. We learned how to upholster seats and make wooden wheels. We decided together when valves were ground shiny enough and if the engine could get by on the original pistons—which it still has.

In the end, poor Mom knew that if I called, she and I would talk two or three minutes and then she would have to say, "I suppose you want to talk to Dad. He's standing right here." You don't know this, but my Dad was the quietest man ever. But we could talk about that old car. In fact, we talked more about that car than we had talked about anything else. Marriage, children, school, moving—nothing compared to talking about the T.

It took four years to get it all done. We spent only $2,000 on the whole restoration by doing everything ourselves. We found parts for what was missing and put together the rear seat, rear doors, and fenders from three different cars. We're not great autobody men, but we learned to hammer out dents well enough. We painted it in our garage—the original black, no more blue. The engine works just fine, starting on the second pull every time. The new upholstery is shiny black, and the wooden wheels we built look great.

Is it perfect? No, not even close. We didn't do a perfect paint job, and thousands of miles of driving with the whole family has taken its toll. The seat springs are a little tired now, the cover for the folding top has a stitched-up tear on the back side, and last Saturday I noticed a nut had vibrated off the dash, leaving a bolt just sticking through. As the old phrase goes, it's a 20/20 car. From 20 feet away going 20 miles an hour, it looks good. But looking perfect was never the point.

Could it look perfect? Sure, perfection is a phone call and credit card away. There are many Model T parts sellers with huge catalogs of Model T parts, and they would be happy to send us a perfect set of fenders to replace the ones we have. They would sell us a new radiator to fix our leaky original. They would send us a completely rebuilt engine, ready to be bolted in. Perfection is right there in the catalog. And we would never have to do a thing ourselves. There are body men happy to paint those new fenders and mechanics who would bolt that new engine in. We could have had it perfect in no time at all.

Your work is the same. You probably didn't restore a Model T with your father, but your family probably went through the same choices. When you were small, you wanted to help in the kitchen. But how much help is a five-year-old standing on a kitchen chair, measuring a cup of sugar, pouring three-fourths of it into the bowl and the rest onto the counter? How much help is it when you give your ten-year-old son a brush and a bucket of paint and aim him toward the garage wall? It makes great pictures, but the wall will definitely need a second coat tomorrow. How daring is it when you give your sixteen-year-old the keys and say, "Here, why don't you drive?" We're not expecting instant perfection. The sugar and paint will be spilled, and we're going to wish we had that extra brake pedal on the passenger side like the drivers-education cars have. But we're nurturing a patient relationship with our child, and that matters more than having instant perfection.

GOD'S CATALOG OF PERFECTION

When we open the Bible, God's catalog, don't we expect instant perfection? Think of Genesis 1 and 2 as the opening pages of a very thick catalog. What sort of work is God doing, and how well is it turning out? The evaluation repeated by God Himself over and over is "And God saw that it was good" (see Genesis 1:4, 10, 12, 18, 21, 25), culminating with "Behold, it was very good" (v. 31). The relatively immediate work of creating through the six days gives instant perfection.

Given this beginning, what do we expect God to do with the rest of the pages of His story, His catalog of work? With every bend in the river, we can't help but expect that the next view will be another scene of His perfection. When He puts His hand to work, what else could He do but perfection? The Psalms especially describe this instant perfection in creation. "Great are the works of the LORD, studied by all who delight in them. Full of splendor and majesty is His work, and His righteousness endures forever" (Psalm 111:2–3). "O LORD, how manifold are Your works!

In wisdom have You made them all; the earth is full of Your creatures" (Psalm 104:24). The perfection of God's power naturally comes with the speed of the Genesis 1 creation.

But then, of course, this simple expectation has to pause and wonder over Genesis 3. Even while we wrestle with the serpent being in the perfect garden, the instant perfection model of God's action suggests that He'll fix the problem right now. One is promised to come to crush the serpent's head (Genesis 3:15). Won't He find the serpent and crush him, just as quickly as He built the whole world? Restore the perfection! Make things as they were.

What Do We Do after the Accident?

After we had the Model T for a few years, I got hit by another car while making a left turn. The T has no turn signals, so you signal with your arm in the old-fashioned method. The man behind me didn't see my arm out and started to pass me as I turned left. Ouch! There went the left front fender, front wheel, and axle. I called Dad, and he loaded up the spare parts that day and left the next morning for Butternut. We worked for two days so that it was as good as ever.

Isn't that what we expect of God when the serpent crashes into Eden? Lord, bring what's needed and get this fixed! This is what we see God do with many of the miracles in both the Old and New Testaments. When there's a crisis, the perfect solution often comes instantly. When the son of the widow dies, Elijah immediately prays fervently over the boy, and the boy is restored that very day (1 Kings 17:17–24). We see this instant perfection especially in Jesus' healings. Peter's mother-in-law is healed of her fever immediately (Mark 1:31), the leper is cleansed instantly (1:42), the paralytic takes up his bed at once (2:12), the withered hand is healed that moment (3:5), and the woman's bleeding is stopped as soon as she touches Jesus (5:29). When God steps among us and promises help, His healing is complete and without delay.

So we naturally look for this same work in our lives. We join Paul in asking for the thorn in the flesh to be taken away today (2 Corinthians 12:7–10). After all, with God, it's not a matter of money or time. Ordering new fenders and an engine is expensive, and there are still a few days in shipping. But what is time and cost to God? He has no budget and no waiting for a check to come in. He has no backlog of work that has to get done first. So why wouldn't He show His power in perfection and do it right now?

GOD'S LOVE OF PATIENCE

Maybe the Model T is the answer. I said that Dad and I could have just ordered all the parts we needed and would have been done. Money was definitely a problem with this idea as we would have quadrupled our expenses at least. Floorboards dragged out from a snowbank cost $10. Perfect ones from the catalog—$180.

But it's more than money. The temperature on the day we got our fenders and running boards was about minus 10 degrees, the dead of winter. Dad and I went to a neighboring farm and hauled these pieces out from under an old semi trailer. We were amazed that we could find running boards, not in a catalog, but in the snowbank under a trailer. Ten dollars was no problem. We retold that story to each other many times. Opening the catalog, getting out the credit card, and then opening a box two days later wouldn't have been the same as shoveling running boards out of the snowbank.

The most important thing of that parts-hunting day and every day we worked was that Dad wanted to do this with me. It's one thing to have a crazy idea yourself: *Let's build a Model T Ford!* But it's another thing to have someone share your idea down to ten below. It's one thing to have the rest of the family ask, back in the warm farmhouse kitchen, "What did you find?" It's another thing for someone to burrow in the snow ahead of you and say, "Danny, look what's here."

Besides the adventure, there's ownership. Our T is not perfect. There's a run in the paint on the left rear quarter panel. The upholstery pleats don't perfectly line up from the seat cushion to the seat back. There's a little oil leak by the transmission housing—though every T leaks some just so you know there's still oil in it. But it's pretty good, and we did it. We made new wooden wheels when the old ones gave out. There aren't many wooden wheelwrights around anymore, and we couldn't find anyone who would share their secrets. So we guessed at how to do it, gave it a try, and those wooden-spoke wheels have been solid and true for twenty-two years now.

But it's another thing to have someone share your idea down to ten below.

So it's not about perfection. If you wanted perfection, you wouldn't pull that chair up to the kitchen counter and hand your five-year-old a measuring cup. You wouldn't send your ten-year-old toward your garage wall with a bucket and brush. Instant perfection isn't your goal.

It's about having a patient relationship. We built the T to build a better relationship. The car was an accessory to what was really going on. Dad and I loved this project and, even more, the time we spent. There was no rush. Get some coffee, enjoy the day, and see how much better we are than before.

Instant perfection is a wonderful expectation of God. But having a patient relationship with us might be His more common response. We cry out, "Lord, save us now! Take this away." He comes with love and puts an arm around our shoulders and says, "Let's take our time." Think of the times God does this biblically and His reasons for saying, "This is going to take time." There are at least four reasons why God repeatedly sets us on the path of patient relationship.

LET'S BRING IN THE WHOLE FAMILY

First, it's about more than one relationship. Through this theme of patient relationship, we're certainly going to learn more of the nature of God. But the relationship circle is wider than that. When we built the Model T, Dad and I weren't the only ones working on it. Holly sewed the vinyl and fabric top together, standing on a step ladder, sewing the kit pieces into a top over eight feet long. Our young son, Steve, was the hammer man. Just a little boy of four or so, Steve came morning after morning into the shop to nail down the upholstery. I held the upholstery tack with needle-nose pliers and pulled the upholstery or trim pieces tight. Steve drove the nails in. It was the same in your family. When you had your five-year-old measuring sugar, the three-year-old was watching and waiting. It's not about just one relationship but about the whole family.

The Bible also shows that cultivating a patient relationship widens the relationship circle. Consider Jairus and the bleeding woman in Mark 5:21–43. Jairus the synagogue ruler had a twelve-year-old daughter about to die. Finding Jesus, he rushed Him back to his house to save his daughter. But along the way, the woman who had suffered bleeding for twelve years touched Jesus, having said to herself, "If I touch even His garments, I will be made well" (Mark 5:28). She touched Him secretly, and "immediately the flow of blood dried up" (Mark 5:29). Here's instant perfection at its best. Jesus also knew instantly that power had gone out from Him and asked who touched Him. It was an invitation for her to show her faith and be confirmed in her healing. After she came forward, Jesus assured her, "Your faith has made you well. Go in peace, and be healed of your disease" (Mark 5:34).

THE SCAFFOLDS MADE YOU LOOK

You've driven by that old two-story house countless times. But today you almost stopped in the road. There were scaffolds lined up on two sides up to the second floor. Most of the old paint was stripped off, and you could see where they were trying out two or three new colors. It must have been a beautiful place when it was new. But now, it's no prizewinner. But someone must have seen potential in it, so the scaffolds went up.

Our world is an old house that, in Eden, was beautiful and perfect. But it's showing its age and wear. But God's amazing patience continues to work on it and us. The Carpenter still builds His house in this world. If you look carefully, you can see the shape of a cross in the scaffolding around a house. That's the shape God chose to show both His patience and His perfection. When you look at your life, don't look only at weathered pieces and mismatched trim. Don't look at what still needs work. Look for the Carpenter, who comes every day and shows His work in the cross. Perfection will come someday, but patience is here every day.

Jairus must have longed for this immediate and perfect healing, but it was taking too long. After all, the woman had been bleeding for twelve years while his daughter was dying that very moment. In fact, his daughter had already died, and the message reached him as they were walking. Jesus said, "Do not fear, only believe" (Mark 5:36). Now the woman's faith became the saving example, not the distraction or delay. Focusing on having a patient relationship widens the circle of faith. Though Jesus didn't say it, clearly the context of Jairus's faith was "Only believe—as this woman did, and look at the healing that came to her."

I like to think that the woman came along with the crowd to Jairus's house and said an encouraging word of faith to Jairus. Imagine her walking with Jairus, saying, "It'll be all right. Just trust

Him." Whether she did or not, Jairus faced the mourning household in the company of Jesus, who assured them that the girl was only sleeping. He brought Jairus and his wife into the girl's room, took her hand, and raised her by saying, "Little girl, I say to you, arise" (Mark 5:41). Immediately she rose, but this immediate moment of perfect health came only after the long walk and Jesus' invitation for Jairus to have a patient relationship of trust on the way.

Having a patient relationship widens our circle of faith. It allows us to see the pattern of faith that others have and to value their experience. Their healing doesn't put them alone at the head of the line. Their healing is visible proof that our faith isn't foolish. And we might also become that picture of faith and patience for someone else, whether we recognize them or not.

I've Got Something for You to Do

The first step in cultivating a patient relationship with someone is to widen the circle of faith and value the faith of others. The second step invites us to get busy. If you order all the parts for your car, you have nothing to do while you wait. You can only sit there watching for the UPS truck to come. But if you are going to do all this yourself, then there's always something needing to be sanded or cleaned. Get busy. Doing is natural. Show a ten-year-old a wall, a brush, and a bucket of paint, and he knows what to do.

When we're in a patient relationship, that relationship gives value to what we can do. When God does all immediately and perfectly, it's a wonderful gift of grace. We are certainly saved entirely by the action of God, nothing of our work, but as a gift (Ephesians 2:8–9). And yet we are also God's workmanship, created for the good works that He has prepared for us to walk in (Ephesians 2:10). That walk is the patient relationship He gives us.

The miraculous healing of Naaman the Syrian shows this patience and the worth of what little can be done. Second Kings 5:1–14 tells of Naaman, the army commander with leprosy who heard that the prophet Elisha could cure his incurable disease. Elisha sent word by a messenger that Naaman should wash seven times in the Jordan. Naaman expected instant perfection. He said, "I thought that he would surely come out to me and stand and call upon the name of the LORD his God, and wave his hand over the place and cure the leper" (2 Kings 5:11). But Naaman was persuaded to go through the patient steps of washing in the Jordan, and he was completely healed.

The miracle is amazing in itself, but it's the patient relationship, the use of the small steps of faith, that stands out. Naaman knew that, in itself, the sevenfold washing would do nothing. But it was not the water but the promise that Elisha made and the faith that followed that brought the miracle. We see this same relationship and use of small actions when Jesus fed the five thousand through the small contribution of the boy's loaves and fish. We also see this patient relationship when Jesus changed water into wine, using the work of the servants who drew the 120 to 180 gallons of water to fill the jars. He is the God who called all things into being by a word and created all from nothing. Yet He uses the creation that is already present—bread, fish, water, and oil—and the acts of faith of those who are being brought into closer relationship.

RUST? NO PROBLEM

A growing patient relationship values what little we can do. But a truly patient relationship is patient even with its enemies. This is the third key to understanding a patient relationship. I grew up with the happy confidence that my Dad could fix anything. I hope you felt the same way. Your Dad fixed the broken bicycle with its snapped chain, bent rim, and flat tire. He got your car running on the side of the road that rainy night. He took you to McDonald's the night Jordan called and said that your relationship was over. Jordan was gone, but Dad was still there, and he even had you laughing a little by the time you finished the fries together.

God's patient relationship with us lets our Father show all that He can do. If we rely on instant perfection only, we'll look for a fix at the first sign of trouble. Instant perfection wants the first ache healed now, the first lean day filled with a cornucopia of food, and the first gray, windy day turned to sunshine before noon. Things would never get out of hand because God would put them right instantly at the first sign of trouble.

But then what would that show of God's real power? And wouldn't trouble itself complain? "You never gave us a real chance! You only fixed the little things." Anybody can wash a new car and make it look good. Let's see what you can do with that beat-down, forsaken Model T. So let the troubles run their course and do all they can. Then when God steps in, it's a complete victory.

> God's patient relationship with us lets our Father show all that He can do.

Perhaps the best example of this is Elijah's contest with the prophets of Baal (1 Kings 18). He challenged the 450 prophets of Baal to call fire down from heaven to consume the sacrifice they prepared. He gave the prophets the whole day to prepare their altar and sacrifice and then to call on their idol. By noon, he mocked them by saying, "Cry aloud, for he is a god. . . . Perhaps he is asleep and must be awakened" (1 Kings 18:27). Though it appeared hopeless, he allowed them several more hours to limp around their sacrifice. When nothing happened, no one could say that they didn't have a chance to do all they could.

Then Elijah called the people near and talked about this patient relationship. "Then Elijah said to all the people, 'Come near to me." And all the people came near to him" (1 Kings 18:30). Even with the immediate power of God waiting to be seen, Elijah carefully repaired the altar of God and took twelve stones for the twelve tribes. He not only prepared the wood and the sacrifice, but he also dug a trench around the sacrifice and soaked the sacrifice, the wood, the altar, and the trench with water. The suspense must have been unbearable. Only at the end, after a day of waiting, did he call for the fire of God. "Answer me, O LORD, answer me, that this people may know that You, O LORD, are God, and that You have turned their hearts back" (1 Kings 18:37). Notice that Elijah didn't ask for merely power, but for the restored relationship with the people of Israel. The fire came and consumed everything, even the water and stones. The people were brought back into a relationship with God, saying, "The LORD, He is God; the LORD, He is God" (1 Kings 18:39).

Elijah moved the tribes of Israel toward a stronger relationship with God through this patient waiting for the miracle. The next chapter shows how important it was for Elijah himself to have a patient relationship with God. After destroying the opposition in one day, Elijah should have been ecstatic. However, when the report of his victory reached Queen Jezebel, she vowed that she'd kill Elijah that day. Elijah, the victor, fled to the desert, despondent and questioning. He complained to God, asking to die, saying, "It is enough; now, O LORD, take away my life, for I am no better than my fathers" (1 Kings 19:4). Elijah likely hoped that his victory would silence Jezebel's threats. But the perfection of fire wasn't enough for the endurance that was needed in the days to come.

Elijah's despair was the perfect opening for God's patience and ongoing relationship. He answered Elijah's complaint by feeding him twice, and in that strength Elijah traveled for forty days. But at the end of that, he renewed his complaint that he was the only one left and his life was in danger. God's patience sent Elijah to the mouth of the cave. Passing before him came a tearing wind, an earthquake, and then a fire. Any of those would have been the immediate perfection and unmistakable power needed against Jezebel. But the Lord was in none of them. Instead, He was in a low whisper. God asked again, "What are you doing here, Elijah?" A third time, Elijah complained that he was the only one left and his life was in danger. But this third time, God answered with the assignment to go back, to the very land of danger, to anoint new kings and prophets. Also, to answer finally Elijah's complaint that he was the only one left, God said there were seven thousand people left who had not fallen to Baal worship.

Elijah's desert experience is a wonderful example of God's patient relationship with us even when instant perfection has not driven all problems from our lives. Certainly the power of fire from heaven should have been more than enough, but how quickly despair came the very next day. So with the threat of death came Elijah's isolation and his presumption that he alone had this dangerous faith. If fire from heaven wouldn't do it, what's the use of living? But God showed His strong preference for patient relationship by allowing Elijah's three-time complaint. He showed His kindness as a Father by providing the food and water needed. God also showed His insight into Elijah's expectation by sending wind, earthquake, and fire as possible signs of His presence. But God subverted Elijah's expectation by being in the still, small voice, the epitome of a patient relationship. That voice showed relationship by giving Elijah work to do. Think about this: you can help your five-year-old better when she's working in the kitchen beside you than when she's alone on the living room couch. So God renewed his tie with Elijah by coming near to him and giving him work to do, by returning Elijah to Himself and anointing him. And as a final reminder of God's patient relationship with Elijah, lest Elijah continue with his litany of solitary woe, God pointed to seven thousand relationships that had not failed.

Let's Start a New One

This renewed relationship with Elijah set the stage for more work and even greater miracles through Elisha. Patient relationships not only welcome years of work, but they're also willing to start the journey all over. This willingness to begin over is the fourth trait of patient relationships. I've mentioned that Dad and I worked on the Model T for four years to get it done. You can probably guess what's next. As we neared the end of the Model T restoration, we heard of a 1930 Ford Model A Tudor Sedan for sale. Like the Model T, it was beaten down. While it had doors, four fenders, a hood, and a complete drivetrain, there was no interior or seats, the roof was only open sky, and the wheels were all from later cars. It was a sad, rusted lump, sitting in a December snowbank.

We bought it, of course. We paid too much for it, $700, but we had high hopes. We didn't have a place for it at home, so for two years we stored and worked on it in a rented brick garage that had no electricity. Our only light came from two small windows and a Coleman camping lantern hissing away. It was often cold and damp. But what great memories were made there. It wasn't about the cold and dark but the chance to start over again and to have more years together.

The Model A took us another four years. But it was more than the time. Model A Sedans are much more complete cars than Model T touring cars. The A was a true car, with a fixed roof, roll-up windows, instruments on a dash, and an electric starter for the engine. (You hand-crank a 1917 Model T engine since electric starters didn't come out on the Model T until 1919.) It all means much more work, more parts, and new things to learn. It was the perfect next step.

Patient relationships build on what we already have and look for a new step, maybe one that is even more challenging. An example of this is the raising of Lazarus in John 11. Mary and

Martha sent word to Jesus that Lazarus was deathly ill. They knew His healing power and had every reason to expect an instant perfection of healing when Jesus heard of Lazarus's illness. He would at least come as soon as possible, and then Lazarus would be well. We can see this expectation in the words that both Martha and Mary each said separately when they met Jesus after Lazarus's death: "Lord, if You had been here, my brother would not have died" (John 11:21, 32). Yet despite this trust, Lazarus died and was buried for four days before Jesus came.

While they could have easily turned to the despair of Elijah, Martha affirmed her faith in Jesus as the resurrection and life (John 11:27). But the sisters faced a greater challenge than any before in Jesus' ministry. While He had resurrected two people already—the daughter of Jairus (Mark 5:35–43) and the son of the widow of Nain (Luke 7:11–16)—both of these were done on the day of the death. This was a much greater challenge as Lazarus had been dead for four days. Death and decay had taken complete hold. However, Jesus reminded Martha, "Did I not tell you that if you believed you would see the glory of God?" (John 11:40). So they took the stone away, an enormous step of faith for the sisters.

This moment of trusting relationship, a relationship tested by questioning days of delay, is balanced by the next words of relationship as Jesus said, "Father, I thank You that You have heard Me. I knew that You always hear Me, but I said this on account of the people standing around, that they may believe that You sent Me" (John 11:41–42). After Jesus had highlighted the perfect relationship between Himself and the Father, it was time for instant perfection. "He cried out with a loud voice, 'Lazarus, come out.' The man who had died came out" (John 11:43–44).

Lazarus's resurrection exceeded the hopes that Martha and Mary had of instant perfection. It was the culmination of the women's trusting, patient relationship with Jesus. It showed that faith is willing to begin at the lowest point and take on challenges that are even greater than the past. A patient relationship can say "Yes, I believe" even when the tombstone hasn't yet moved.

Besides showing the faithful patience of Mary and Martha, Jesus' raising of Lazarus highlighted His relationship as the beloved Son of God. This relationship was further expressed by the aftermath of Lazarus's resurrection. The unmistakable power of Jesus' work became the talk of Jerusalem (John 11:45; 12:9–10). Because this miracle couldn't be denied, Jesus' popularity grew so that the high priest developed the plot to kill Him (John 11:49–53). This crucifixion would result in Jesus' final words of commitment to the Father's care, "Father, into Your hands I commit My spirit" (Luke 23:46). This perfect relationship of the Father and Son was especially shown after the patient wait of three days, Good Friday to Easter. But on Easter morning, "[He] was declared to be the Son of God in power according to the Spirit of holiness by His resurrection from the dead" (Romans 1:4). The instant perfection of the resurrection is the affirming stamp of the eternal relationship of Father and Son.

> A patient relationship can say "Yes, I believe" even when the tombstone hasn't yet moved.

More Wrinkles Than Promises, More Memories Than Hopes

This interplay of the themes of instant perfection and patient relationship is the basis for many of the biblical themes that follow. You've noticed that it shares the dual nature of some of the other themes such as "It's Not the First but the Second That Counts" and "What Does Greatness Look Like?" This dual nature is in line with much of the nature of Lutheran theology with a stress on the Law and Gospel as divinely coordinated elements of God's message. It also matches the Lutheran emphasis on Jesus' incarnation as fully divine and fully human, a complete incarnation that continues still today. This incarnation allows for Lutherans to stress the Sacrament of the Lord's Supper as both bread and wine along with the real presence of the Lord's body and blood. In short, much of Lutheran theology mirrors the both-and relationship shown in the themes of instant perfection and patient relationship.

We see a combination of both instant perfection and patient relationship in our life of faith as well as in our reading of Scripture. Unquestionably, God is powerful enough to provide instant perfection. He is able to do far more abundantly than all we ask or imagine (Ephesians 3:20–21). As Paul prayed for the removal of the thorn in the flesh (2 Corinthians 12:7–8), we can ask for the instant work of God's power. This isn't a challenge against God, a dare we throw at Him. We're asking for relief by all His power. We're the people praying for Peter's release from prison (Acts 12:12–17), and look, Peter was immediately led out that same night by an angel.

But what if there is no instant perfection? What if our life is more the past than the future? What if we have more wrinkles than promises, more memories than hopes? The patient relationship that God extends is not a consolation prize, a small thing thrown our way when perfection can't come. It can be the greatest gift, the patient relationship of God with fallen people. We have to cry with Paul in Romans 7 that the good we would do we don't, and the evil we hate we still do. And yet, He remains with us. We were a weight of death upon Him, yet He patiently remained with us to the end. Dad didn't come to work with me on the Model A in a bright, warm garage. He worked for days in a cold, damp place. Now that's a patient relationship. It wasn't the car, the garage, or the work that brought Dad over. It was being together that filled those days.

So God remains with us, saying, "I came for you." He didn't come for what He could get from us or for the power He would show. He didn't come simply to display instant perfection and be done with the job. Heaven displays instant and eternal perfection.

On earth, He shows patient relationship above all. He came for the tie between us. He joined our lives with Himself in Baptism, making us one with Him in death and resurrection so that our life is now hidden with His (Romans 6:3–4).

Back to the Model T. Dad's working days went away along with his sight, but we remembered it all. The snowbanks got a bit deeper in our memory and, say, I think it was maybe 15 degrees below that day we found the running boards. We remembered how dark that rented garage was and how we got the Model T running for the first time on Father's Day. The Model T is still in our garage today, and it still starts on the second pull of the crank. It never was perfect, but the memories are. We built a Model T, and that T built a good part of us.

Think of all God is building with you. Every day could be a display of instant perfection, and all thanks to Him when that comes. But at the end of many more days, when nothing seems to have gotten done and every problem is just as hard as ever, we can wonder what good ever happened. God puts an arm around our shoulders and says, "Well, we worked on your patience, didn't we?" And it's the "we" that matters. As He shows repeatedly in the lives of biblical people, in the anxious waiting of Jairus and the daring trust of Elijah, God most often works through a patient relationship with us. We build a lifetime of patient trust, and His patience builds us.

> God puts an arm around our shoulders and says, "Well, we worked on your patience, didn't we?"

"ABIDE WITH ME"

A hymn that captures our yearning for a patient relationship with God is certainly "Abide with Me" by Henry F. Lyte (*LSB* 878). While all the stanzas speak of this relationship, three stand out. Though Jesus could come in an instant with an unbearable perfection, stanza 3 speaks of Him as the patient Friend of sinners:

> Come not in terrors, as the King of kings,
>
> But kind and good, with healing in Thy wings;
>
> Tears for all woes, a heart for ev'ry plea,
>
> Come, Friend of sinners, thus abide with me.

Because of this patient relationship, we live in present and future faith. Faith in His promises see an instant perfection of the resurrection coming. Stanza 5 describes this:

> I fear no foe with Thee at hand to bless;
>
> Ills have no weight and tears no bitterness,
>
> Where is death's sting? Where, grave, thy victory?
>
> I triumph still if Thou abide with me!

We began our biblical journey with the instant perfection of Eden, but we hope for more than a return to Eden. We're ready to put this world away and see a new, lasting perfection come, all by the eternal relationship founded on the cross. Stanza 6 sums all this up:

> Hold Thou Thy cross before my closing eyes;
>
> Shine through the gloom, and point me to the skies,
>
> Heav'n's morning breaks, and earth's vain shadows flee:
>
> In life, in death, O Lord, abide with me.

DISCUSSION QUESTIONS

1. You likely haven't restored a Model T Ford, but you have worked long and hard on a project. What have you worked on that's taken a long time and made a closer tie between you and someone else?

2. This chapter discussed several times when God has brought out instant perfection. Why does instant perfection make perfect sense as the hallmark of God?

3. How and why are we more likely to pray for an instant-perfection answer from God rather than one of patient relationship?

4. Having a patient relationship with God is a two-way street. First, how does God show His remarkable patience in biblical accounts and also in His relationship with us?

5. Second, how does having a patient relationship with God draw us toward a greater measure of patience with God? Is there a biblical person who embodies that patience toward God?

6. Patience generally waits for something. If we are in a patient relationship with God, what are some of the things, events, and changes for which we're waiting?

7. On the other hand, having a patient relationship with God can be an end in itself. How is having a patient relationship with God our ultimate life goal?

CHAPTER 3

It's Not the First but the Second That Counts

Remember your first job? Maybe you ran the front counter at McDonald's, stocked shelves at the Piggly Wiggly grocery store, or washed dishes at the food service at college. You probably remember most the things that went with the work. Who came up with that silly-looking uniform? And you really did have to wear the hat, even when people you knew were going to see you. And who knew this place was open Friday nights and you would get that shift? It was a job to remember and a job to leave.

Work has probably gotten better since your first job. Maybe now you're giving the new employee talk instead of hearing it. Maybe you don't have to wear a silly hat like you did back then. And you probably know what to do every day instead of just trying to look busy. Yes, your new job is all the better given what you went through with the first.

This first/second experience has happened over and over for you. Your first car was a Chevy Cavalier that cost you $63. I know a young man who actually drove that car through high school. A $63 Chevy is no prizewinner, but at least you won't be asked to give anyone a ride in it. Your first apartment—remember that place? On the second floor, no elevator, no air conditioning, and the water never stopping running in the bathroom sink. That matched the puddle of water under the fridge every morning. But by now, I hope that the only thing you have from that first car is the key you kept when it was sent to the crusher. That apartment is only a faded photo in your memory. You're doing much better now.

That's our theme: it's not the first but the second that counts. This theme is largely the mirror opposite of our first theme, "Instant Perfection—Patient Relationship." There we began with what's perfect and expected that it would continue. Here we start with what we quickly know is not the answer. But we live in patience with the first step since we believe that a second is coming. The second will not necessarily be perfect, as many biblical people quickly show. But there is a clear step forward from the first to the second if we have the patience to see it.

IT'S HIS CHOICE, NOT OURS

Where were you born in your family? We don't choose to be born either first, second, third, or thirteenth. But God does often choose a biblical pattern by which the first is often quickly followed by a second. And that second has blessings and benefits that the first didn't receive. This doesn't mean that the first is useless or that all of life has to follow this pattern. Don't get divorced just so you can say, "I got through the first marriage so I could get to the second." However, there are many examples of God's special use for and blessings upon the second.

This pattern can be easiest to see in the lives of biblical people. I suspect you're already thinking of the classic pair, Esau and Jacob. God already distinguished these two twin brothers before birth. "Two nations are in your womb, and two peoples from within you shall be divided; the one shall be stronger than the other, the older shall serve the younger" (Genesis 25:23). God's choice came before they had done anything to deserve blessing or woe. As we know, Jacob, the second to be born, lived a tension-filled life, at times receiving due justice for his selfishness and at other times getting blessings beyond deserving. God's choice of Jacob made him the one who received the name *Israel*, "the one who wrestles with God" (see Genesis 32:28). Jacob also was the final name by which God defined Himself when He said that He was the God of Abraham, Isaac, and Jacob (Exodus 3:6).

We Might as Well Go So We Can Come Back

My father was a very quiet man who loved to stay home. After working in the shop, fields, and barn all day, he wanted only to sit in his chair at night, watch *Gunsmoke* or *Bonanza*, and go to sleep early. But my mother loved to visit people. So they had a compromise: they would go visiting the relatives at night if Mom promised they would leave early. Dad would then say, "We might as well go so we can come back." In fact, Dad was hoping something like this: "If I suggest we go really early, maybe we won't have to go at all." It never worked out that way, but he was hoping.

We might be tempted in this theme to be just as rushed as Dad. Let's just race through the first thing so we can get to the second. But we can't skip the first because that first person, place, or action has, in itself, a crucial part of the message. A brief example would be the sequence of prophets leading to the Son of God in Hebrews 1:1–2: "Long ago, at many times and in many ways, God spoke to our fathers by the prophets, but in these last days He has spoken to us by His Son." We certainly are anxious to hear the distinctive words of the Son, but the Old Testament as a whole and especially the voices of the prophets have to be heard first. Knowing their message, we can recognize and appreciate the words of the Son.

So while we naturally focus on Jacob as the second one, there was also a role for Esau as the first. The brothers were apart for years. Esau's welcome of Jacob leaves every reader holding his breath. Jacob was frightened before the meeting and sent the gifts and his family forward first to soften Esau. But despite the gifts, we have every reason to expect that Esau will finally get his revenge on Jacob for stealing their father's blessing. Instead, Esau showed a graciousness that reflected God's mercy (Genesis 33:10). Esau was not the blessed second, but he became the first who conveyed a blessing.

God chose Jacob as the favored second one, so we'd rightly expect that this same pattern of favoring the second would be repeated in his life. One of the most striking instances is his marriages to the two sisters Leah and Rachel. Since we've just come from the tension of the twin brothers Esau and Jacob, it's not surprising that immediately upon fleeing home, Jacob met Rachel and soon after her sister Leah. In a double way, our principle of "It's Not the First but the Second That Counts" works out here. Jacob met Rachel first and certainly fell in love. He proposed marriage, and the wedding was set. We seem to

> Esau was not the blessed second, but he became the first who conveyed a blessing.

be on a simple, one-person track. But it was not the first sister that he met that counted; it was the second, Leah, who was the first married to Jacob. Of course, we might also see the principle work in terms of Jacob's affection when, after he married Rachel a week later, he continued to love her, the second wife and the younger sister, more. This same pattern of rivalry continues in this family, of first and second to bear children and the preference shown to the younger sons. Overall, the pattern of preference for the second lived in this family, but it didn't guarantee peace for them.

Another time when two sons follow this pattern but with an interesting twist in birth order is the parable of the prodigal son in Luke 15. We are conditioned by this point in reading the Bible to expect that the younger of the two sons would be the more important character in the parable. And the younger son certainly became the center of the story when he left home, wasted his father's money, despaired, and returned to his father. The younger son filled the stage, and the older appeared forgotten. But not by the father. We might have wondered why the father in the parable never pursued his lost son, especially since the shepherd and the woman in the previous parables of chapter 15 immediately searched for the lost lamb and coin. The father waited for the younger son to come. But it was not only this first lost son that counted but also the second lost son who had to be sought.

The father left the celebration and searched for his older son. He couldn't celebrate unless he found the older son. When we would have simply ended the story with the prodigal's return, the final key to the parable is the father seeking the older son.

David's children are another example of this theme. First, we expect that David will have children who follow his example as a man after God's own heart. Especially, we're looking for a son who will succeed him as king. For that, he needed the right wife. I've always thought that Abigail would have been the perfect wife and mother. Remember Abigail? In 1 Samuel 25, David sent messengers to ask Nabal, Abigail's husband, to share some of the produce of his flock in thanks for David's protection. But Nabal, a fool equal to his name, refused to give anything. David and four hundred of his men charged down the mountain to kill Nabal and any man in his camp. Abigail heard of all this, immediately prepared a feast for David's men, and met David, putting the blame entirely on herself for not knowing of David's request. Of course, she was innocent, but her courage and grace turned David back. Ten days later, Nabal died, and soon thereafter David married Abigail.

While David did have other wives, wouldn't Abigail have been the perfect match for David? Surely her son should have been the next king. But we hear nothing more of her after the marriage. Instead, we all know the next wife of David, Bathsheba. Who would have thought that Bathsheba would be the mother of the king? But that again was the remarkable choice of God. Furthermore, it was not the first son of Bathsheba and David that became king. As you remember, their first son died soon after Nathan the prophet confronted David about his sin with Bathsheba (2 Samuel 12:13–14). We would expect that these two, David and Bathsheba, given their adulterous beginning and the death of their son, would never have children again. But it was not the first but the second son that mattered. David and Bathsheba had a second son, Solomon, the wisest man who ever lived.

In this long series of firsts and seconds, we naturally focus on Solomon. However, both sons of David and Bathsheba had vital roles. Solomon obviously had a crucial job both as the epitome of wisdom and as an expression of the greatness expected of the kingdom. But the firstborn son, the son of the king, who died innocently, had perhaps an even greater importance. He reminds us of the greater Son of David, who died truly innocently on the cross. His death took away all sins of all people and opened the door for all blessings to come.

God's choice of the second son, Solomon, for blessings is echoed in another choice within a tension-filled family. In Luke 10:38–42, Martha and her sister Mary were hosting Jesus at their home. We can only imagine Martha's energy and good intentions. This would be her best meal and finest hour. But we can also easily imagine her increasing frustration as, while she worked alone, her sister Mary sat serenely listening to Jesus. Finally, after glaring looks and muttered hints had done nothing, Martha said to Jesus, "Lord, do You not care that my sister has left me to serve alone?" (Luke 10:40). But Jesus calmed her by repeating her name, "Martha, Martha." He had to say it twice, perhaps because the first time He said it, she barely listened. Getting her attention, Jesus then contrasted the two choices made by Mary and Martha: "You are anxious and troubled about many things, but one thing is necessary. Mary has chosen the good portion, which will not be taken away from her" (Luke 10:41–42). With Martha, we see the choice of hard and generous work, expecting that to be the only option. But it's not the first choice but the second, Mary's, that counts.

In Martha's case, it took Jesus' own words to show the better, second choice. However, sometimes the first one knows his role is just that, the first, and that the second is the one that counts. John the Baptist was a perfect example of this. He was the long-awaited messenger, the forerunner of Jesus who prepared the way as predicted in Isaiah 40 and fulfilled in Mark 1:4–8. John knew his role, as he said, "You yourselves bear me witness, that I said, 'I am not the Christ, but I have been sent before Him.'... He must increase, but I must decrease" (John 3:28, 30). John was the necessary messenger, the voice in the wilderness, but he was ready to step off the stage when the mature ministry of Jesus began.

THIS WILL TAKE TIME

And so, in these many examples of relationships, we see how especially extended family members live out this principle of first and second. However, it is not always a simple preference given to the younger, though Jacob and Solomon certainly exemplify this. The pattern of first/second can be seen in a range of relationships and sequences. The first is important, but keep your eye on what happens even more to the second. This focus on the second is convenient for our reading. We can easily ask, "Here is the first, so what will the second do that's even more?" And we are rarely disappointed.

However, the turn from the first to the second isn't always quickly done. You saw that in your own life. You knew that first car wasn't much and would have been happy to trade up after only a week. But there was no chance. So you endured the first clunky car, lived in that first terrible apartment for two years, and worked that first job even if you hated it. Change was coming, but at the time you couldn't quite see it. The second may have counted, and you were counting on it, but the first certainly took its time.

So also, we have a wide range of first/second examples that span much more time than the lives of siblings or the change from one generation to another. Often this change comes with the exchange of one person's life for another, whether those lives touched each other or were hundreds of years apart. Also this greater span between first and second is found especially with the replacement of one

> The second may have counted, and you were counting on it, but the first certainly took its time.

object or location with another. As we meet the first half of the principle in these cases, we need both good memories and patience to wait for the greater step to come.

A Second Serving and More

If the first movie in a series has car chases and crashes, the second movie has more. If the first movie happens in an exotic setting, the second won't be in your backyard. If the first movie puts the hero in near-fatal danger, it will only get worse for him in the second. It's a guarantee that the essence of the first movie will grow in the second.

Biblically, we can see this same increase of the essential actions of one man leading to the next generation. One of the clearest examples of two generations with this increase is Elijah and Elisha, the miracle-working prophets of 1 and 2 Kings. Elijah was the bold prophet who confronted King Ahab with the contest of calling fire from heaven as a challenge to the 450 prophets of Baal (1 Kings 18). Elijah lived through the famine with the widow because by God's miracle her flour and oil never ran out. He also raised the son of the widow from the dead. Finally, he was taken into heaven directly by the horses and chariots of fire.

As dramatic as these events were, Elisha inherited a double measure of Elijah's spirit (2 Kings 2:9–12). The miracles God worked through Elisha might be accounted as a double measure in many ways. Elisha promised the barren Shunammite woman a son, and then he raised that son from the dead (2 Kings 4:8–37). He didn't bring about a daily measure of oil and flour for three people as Elijah did, but he provided the miracle of the widow's oil that didn't stop until it paid all her debts (2 Kings 4:1–7). He not only healed the leprosy of Naaman the Syrian but then transferred the disease to his greedy servant Gehazi (2 Kings 5:1–27). He blinded the entire army of the Syrians and then led them out of Israel (2 Kings 6:8–23). Even after Elisha's death, a dead man came to life simply by being placed in the grave with Elisha (2 Kings 13:21). In the sequence of Elijah to Elisha, the promise of a double measure of his spirit became clear with these multiplied miracles. If the two prophets were a pair of movies, then *Elisha: The Sequel* would certainly promise more action than ever before.

THE SECOND DOOR IS THE ONE YOU WANT

Winter shows it best. Which door to a house actually gets used? The front door is impressive and has a doorbell and knocker. That seems the obvious choice. But notice, the snow is untouched in front of it. Around the side, almost hidden, is the service door to the garage. There's no doorbell and no stained glass there, but the tracks in the snow show this is the door you want to use. When you don't know the family, you have to start with the front door. But once you're a part of the family, come in through the side.

Many of our examples of the first are like the impressive front door. Saul, the first king, stands taller than all others. The first Jerusalem temple was magnificent. But the second choice was the one that counted. David, small shepherd though he was, was the doorway for the house God proposed to build. The true dwelling place of God was through the body of the Carpenter from Nazareth. Don't stop at the front door only. Look around the corner and see the second door that perhaps only the family members know and use.

CROSSING THE MIGHTY MAC

I rode my motorcycle over the Mackinac Bridge, the Mighty Mac, yesterday. That's the bridge that connects the upper and lower peninsulas of Michigan. It is a magnificent bridge, some five miles long with two suspension towers, each tower being 552 feet above the water. The bridge's roadway itself is 200 feet above the water. The bridge spans over the union of Lake Michigan and Lake Huron. They say that the view from the highest part of the bridge is tremendous. I wouldn't know. I'm afraid of heights, so yesterday on a motorcycle on a windy day, I was watching the road and only the road. I looked at pictures online today to see what I missed. Julius Caesar may have traveled by these words: I came, I saw, I conquered. My trip over the bridge was more like this: I went, I whimpered, I wobbled my way to the other side.

The key to riding over the bridge is to count the two towers and the curved middle of the bridge between them. It's really an exercise in patience and perfection. The bridge is fine. Over 150 million vehicles have gone over it. I think it can take my Yamaha FJR 1300 and me. But it's about patience. Due to repairs, one lane was closed, and we went over mostly on the lane of steel grating that shook my bike side to side. The speed limit was twenty miles per hour due to loaded trucks in the lane. So as much as I wanted to be done with this, I had to be patient, go slow, and hold on. The key was to get to the first tower but then keep going.

I went, I whimpered, I wobbled my way to the other side.

You're not allowed to stop on the bridge, so getting to the first tower is just the start. The tower leads you to the steep climb of the middle span. Keep climbing over the curved span, and that leads you to the second tower. Hurrah, now you're on the way down—slowly—to the solid ground of the upper peninsula. The key is the pair of towers with a shared middle span of the bridge, the highest point. In our next first/second pair, we have the same relationship. We are ultimately going to join two pairs together because between them there is a shared high middle ground.

Doing this double connection means we'll span both Old and New Testaments, the lower and upper peninsulas of the Bible so to speak. To cover such a span of time, we'll need people whose names, actions, and characteristics are so striking that we can recall them from one Bible book to another, from one Testament to another. To make that large of a bridge, let's start with a pair that spans two generations and then sets the stage for an Old Testament to New Testament connection. For that, we have perhaps the most promising name in Scripture: Joshua.

Does your name have special meaning? Were you given that name as a way to honor a grandparent? My mother wanted to call me Fred in honor of my grandfather. That would have been okay, but I'm glad Dad stepped in and said that I would be Danny instead. Was your name a way for your parents to chart your future? Call a girl Hope or Joy and trust that her life will be filled with the same.

But what if your name conveyed the promise of salvation? Now that would be a burden. The name *Joshua* means "Yahweh/ the LORD saves" (Numbers 13:16). It might be surprising that the name and role of Savior didn't come with Moses. He, after all, was the one to rescue Israel from Egypt. Moses also saved Israel from the destruction God threatened when they repeatedly rebelled. But the work of Moses was only the first. He brought them to the brink of the Jordan, but he couldn't enter the land or lead them to it. Much like the later forerunning work of John the Baptist, he could come to the Jordan, but that was the high point of his leading.

Another was needed to bring the people into the Promised Land. What a contrast between Moses and Joshua in this leading. When God called him to serve, Moses had to go back to Egypt, the land he left forty years before and must have vowed he would never enter again. But when the leadership role came to Joshua, he had to lead the people forward to the Promised Land. It was a land he had been in before as one of the twelve spies, but a land unknown to the people. In crossing the Red Sea, Moses had to wait all night as the Lord sent a strong east wind to divide the waters, making the sea dry ground, all the while exercising great patience while Pharaoh's army was coming behind them. Joshua, in crossing the Jordan, saw no hint of a miracle until the priests stepped into the floodwaters, and only then did the waters part instantly. In this contrast of patience and perfection, Moses and Joshua are a balanced pair.

But consider what this sequence means as one replaces another. Remember getting a job where you took over for someone, someone who had been there forever and was the expert? That's frightening. I would guess you just wanted to get through the day without major mistakes. But what if you had to take over for someone who worked for forty years and your assignment was to finish their work? Do the job they never did—and have thousands of people watching you try? That was Joshua's challenge, to lead the people beyond where Moses had stopped.

Moses is our first tower who leads to Joshua who then leads the people over the long span of the Lord's salvation. Moses begins the journey by leading Israel from the safe bank of slavery into the unknown of the exodus. But Joshua's leadership promises more. When you pass the first tower on the Mackinac Bridge, you can't see what is coming as the road is still going up. You can only trust that what is coming will hold you and is worth the climb. So we move from Moses to the promise of Joshua, the high span of God's salvation.

It is quite easy to see this first/second relationship with Moses and Joshua as they overlap each other. However, we might also extend the first/second connection with a new pairing, that of Joshua leading to Jesus. The high middle ground of Joshua can't end in itself. Imagine the Mackinac Bridge with only one tower and a middle span that just ends in midair. It needs another anchor and support. So Joshua begins a new first/second sequence, just as the high span of the bridge leads to the second tower.

Joshua was certainly important for Israel's entry to the Promised Land, but it is the coming Savior who is important for us all. Matthew 1:21 records the angel's message that Joseph is to call his son Jesus since He will save His people from their sins. While Joshua's name and work in the Old Testament pointed to the Lord as salvation, Jesus Himself is that Savior. The tie between the two names is close, so much so that the name *Jesus* in the Greek New Testament is identical in spelling to that of *Joshua* in Acts 7:45 and Hebrews 4:8. Joshua's name in the Old Testament pointed to the high span of God's saving work, but the weight of that span rests on Jesus. Within that contrast, what wonderful parallels lie between Jesus and Joshua. Both began their adult ministry of leadership at the Jordan River. For both, there was a significant miracle at the Jordan. For Joshua, the river water parted; for Jesus, the heavens parted at His Baptism. Both led the people to the Promised Land: Joshua taking the people forward into the land and Jesus assuring all believers that in His Father's house there are many rooms and that He has gone to prepare a place there for us and will return to take us to Himself (John 14:1–4). Both followed the significant ministry of another, Moses and John the Baptist, respectively. As we expect, Jesus here is the greater second, the true Savior, previewed by the work of Joshua.

With Moses, we have the beginning of the journey, the uplifting of the first tower. But the journey had to go beyond Moses, and so it did with Joshua. His work of entering the Promised Land led beyond Moses and completed the exodus journey. But the name *Joshua* is a high span of hope that had to be carried by a greater One. When you are at the peak of the bridge, the best sight is the second tower and the graceful sweep of the bridge taking you to land. So Jesus carries the full weight of our hope and without fail leads us home.

It's a Fixer-Upper, a Starter House

We watch a fair amount of HGTV at our house. I've seen near countless episodes of unpermitted additions being pulled down, 1950s cabinets being sledgehammered, and rotten siding getting thrown into a dumpster. A theme in many of these shows is that this place is just a starter home, a bit small and needing a whole new look along with an addition. The story is not about the place as you found it but what you did to remodel.

The Mackinac Bridge is a good image for our first/second theme, the bridge being a model for the three-people sequence of Moses, Joshua, and Jesus. But we can also talk about a building, like a starter house, as a biblical first/second sequence. This building will have an initial simple pairing with a final more elaborate summary.

The tent of meeting is our first. Moses pitched a tent outside the camp during the exodus where God would speak with him while the pillar of cloud would stand at the entrance of the tent (Exodus 33:7–10). It was a wonderful example of a place of worship and meeting, a place where "The LORD used to speak to Moses face to face, as a man speaks to his friend" (Exodus 33:11).

But this first had a much larger and more elaborate second, the tabernacle. Moses was given the directions for a much larger tent, the tabernacle, made by the people's expensive contributions of gold, silver, bronze, brooches, earrings, rings, purple and scarlet yarns, linens, and leather (Exodus 35:21–24). The elaborate tabernacle held the ark of the covenant and the altar and table with the grain offering (Exodus 40:18–30). This second tent is much more what we expect, a greatness that attempts to reflect the glory of God and also expresses the thankful gifts of the people.

This initial sequence of first to second, tent of meeting to tabernacle, prepares us for the next step. Once you've remodeled that first starter house, perhaps you're looking to do another. So also we have the sequence of tabernacle to temple. David brought this contrast to light when he said to Nathan the prophet, "Behold, I dwell in a house of cedar, but the ark of the covenant of the LORD is under a tent" (1 Chronicles 17:1). David expected that the tabernacle was merely a beginning and that a permanent dwelling was needed. A house would be a more appropriate setting for

God's ark. Interestingly, Paul used this same contrast in another first/second sequence when he reminded us that now we live in our bodies like a tent, but in heaven we will live in the resurrected body, compared to a house not built by human hands (2 Corinthians 5:1–4). So the first, the temporary nature of the tent, calls for a more lasting second, the house.

God told David that he would not be the one to build God a house and that God had no need of such a house. In essence, God said, "Don't pity Me, David." In fact, God said that He would build David a lasting house and throne, doing so through David's ultimate Son, Jesus (1 Chronicles 17:4–14). But the appeal of a lasting, physical house was still there for David, who was allowed to gather the materials so that his son Solomon could build the temple. While the tabernacle was an expression of the richness of the people during the exodus, it was nothing compared to the size and grandeur of the temple (2 Chronicles 3–5). This makes a natural, expected pair of first/second steps, tent to tabernacle, tabernacle to temple. In each pair, the first is important and functional, but what counts is the second.

We can extend this pair even further with two more steps. The first temple was destroyed by the Babylonians in 587 BC, and the second temple was built in 516 BC. This second temple, often called Zerubbabel's temple, was built on the foundation of Solomon's temple but was less impressive (Ezra 3–6). Herod the Great enlarged and beautified the temple, and it was that building into which Jesus was brought, where He taught, and which He cleansed. Jesus' presence in the second temple is the reason it was more significant than Solomon's temple. In this second temple, Jesus completed this first/second sequence when He said, "Destroy this temple, and in three days I will raise it up" (John 2:19). Jesus was speaking of His own body as the ultimate temple. Jesus was the end point for this sequence, and what a journey it was: the tent of meeting led to the elaborate tabernacle, the tabernacle led to the magnificent first temple, the first temple was destroyed and rebuilt to the second temple in which Jesus conducted His ministry, and finally the physical second temple was outdone by the living temple of Jesus' body. While the second temple was destroyed in AD 70 and has never been rebuilt, the true temple, Jesus' body, was raised on Easter to life unending. In that temple of His body, we have an eternal meeting place with God.

WHY START ALL OVER?

The bushes on the east side of our house seemed fine when you first saw them. But they grew like mad all summer. Every two weeks, we beat them back by clipping the new shoots. Over six feet tall, they had devoured the gas meter and pipes living behind them. No summer's drought stunted their growth. And no winter snow load could bend them.

They had to go. They were just too tall, too wide, and too dull. So one 90-degree day, I cut them down with my Sawzall and grubbed out the roots. We dug up the ground and put in four hydrangeas. They were only about a foot tall when we put them in, and they didn't come close to hiding the gas meter. They were perfect.

Perfect if you have patience. That was about four years ago, and the hydrangeas are now a wall of blooming white flowers, four feet tall, better looking than that hedge ever was. The change didn't look like much at first as we went from living bushes to bare dirt. But give those hydrangeas time, and see how much better they are.

Our final first/second sequence has some of this same change and surprise to it. Most of our examples have shown a good beginning with a better ending. We've gone from strength to strength. The second is better, more desired, in ways that we can see. Jacob marries Leah first but can't wait to marry Rachel second. But there is a wonderful example of a second that comes as a surprise that is seriously questioned. Only time reveals the value of this choice.

What made someone a disciple, a first-century member of the Twelve who followed Jesus? The disciples had to ask this when they needed a new member to replace Judas. Their solution was in the qualifications they specified: "So one of the men who have accompanied us during all the time that the Lord Jesus went in and out among us, beginning from the Baptism of John until the day He was taken up from us—one of these men must become with us a witness to His resurrection" (Acts 1:21–22). This definition seems completely reasonable. To be a witness of Jesus, you had to have known Jesus, have seen all that He did from the very beginning, and believe that He is the Son of God risen from the dead.

That definition worked well for the Twelve as they had two men to choose from, and Matthias became the new twelfth apostle (Acts 1:26). But that was only the first definition of an apostle. It filled the vacancy of Judas, and it completed the expected number twelve. Yet for all this, Matthias is never heard of again. But a new apostle, sprung from a second definition of apostle, was about to come. He would turn the world upside down and have a name never forgotten.

> He would turn the world upside down and have a name never forgotten.

Saul the Pharisee planned to tear down the growing hedge of the Early Christian Church. He approved of the death of Stephen and was commissioned by the Jerusalem leadership to pursue Christians as far as Damascus. He was the sharp Sawzall, eager to take down anyone in his path. But Jesus' blinding call on the Damascus road turned him. After his three days of blindness and then Baptism by Ananias, Saul began to preach the very Jesus he had once tried to destroy (Acts 9:1–22). He was a completely new definition of an apostle, as they said with wonder as Paul summarized it in Galatians: "They only were hearing it said, 'He who used to persecute us is now preaching the

> He was the sharp Sawzall, eager to take down anyone in his path.

faith he once tried to destroy'" (Galatians 1:23). Paul summed up his unique status as an apostle when he listed himself as the last to whom Jesus appeared after the resurrection: "Last of all, as to one untimely born, He appeared also to me. For I am the least of the apostles, unworthy to be called an apostle, because I persecuted the church of God" (1 Corinthians 15:8–9).

Certainly Paul was the most unlikely apostle, a violent enemy of the faith. But he came about through a gracious definition of apostle. The first definition that brought Matthias was entirely reasonable and focused on Matthias's experiences and support of the faith. But Paul became the second replacement, the unexpected thirteenth, the one admitted not for his past but entirely despite his past. Only the complete grace and power of God would find and raise him up as the greater second.

> The unexpected thirteenth, the one admitted not for his past but entirely despite his past.

Patience Wasn't in the Contract

Paul became the preeminent missionary of the first century, but that didn't happen until he had spent some seventeen years in preparation for his missionary work (Galatians 1:18; 2:1). The time of waiting wasn't likely seen during those three days of blindness in Damascus or in the first days of preaching. Perhaps Paul welcomed the time spent, or maybe he couldn't see the purpose of waiting.

It was likely so for you in the waiting you've done. The first job likely didn't have this line in the contract: "You will be given ample chances to develop patience. In fact, patience may be the only thing you'll take from this job." While you worked through the first job, the pay was soon gone, but I trust that at least some of the patience has remained.

The first/second sequence builds patience above all. Perhaps this is one reason God uses this pattern so often. It brings patience by waiting through the first step in the sequence. That patience can be challenged by what comes next or by the delay in a satisfying second step. Patience might be especially tested when the second step appears, but it's not an instantly recognized perfection. But give God time, and see what He will make of the second when it comes.

Jairus is a good example of this need for patience when going from first to second. In Mark 5, Jairus, the synagogue ruler, urgently asked Jesus to come with him to heal his twelve-year-old daughter who was dying. Jesus went along, and we can imagine Jairus hurrying as fast as he could. But then it all stopped when Jesus met the second one in need. The woman who had been bleeding for twelve years slipped up to Jesus and touched Him, knowing that when she did so, she would be healed. Jesus stopped, asked who touched Him, and then reassured her that her faith had saved her.

I imagine Jairus was frantically saying to himself and maybe others, "But I was first!" Indeed, he was first, but it was not the first to come that received healing but the second. The woman came without credentials of importance. Yet, though her illness would not be fatal that day, still she was healed first.

That made Jairus second, and being second brought a more amazing miracle. It began with faith and patience. Jairus was told after the woman's healing that his daughter had died. But Jesus said, "Do not fear, only believe" (Mark 5:36). It was as if Jesus were saying, "Jairus, look at the faith of the woman and see what was done for her. Believe that this delay with her had a purpose, not only for her, but also for you. Though you were first, she was second, and her healing came first. But remember, the healing of her bleeding was first, an impressive miracle, but the resurrection of your daughter will be the even greater second miracle." We can imagine the woman walking along with Jairus, telling him, "Just trust Him. It will be all right."

This value of patience may be the most important part of this biblical theme. Accept the first step as needed and trust that the second is coming. Another benefit might be the value of the first step itself. I presented this idea some years ago to a group of Lutheran schoolteachers, many of whom were in their first school and first years of teaching. They found great hope in this sequence. They all agreed that the second year of teaching was much easier than the first, of course. But they also saw the value of the first year and that first school overall. We spoke of slowing down their drive to find a brighter class, a bigger room, and a wealthier school. I told them those might come in time. But in the meantime, they should remember that God had a purpose for the class they were in. When He was ready, God could move them on to the second room and school, but they should trust Him in the first.

The first has its time and place, but have faith because a second is coming. That $63 Chevy you first drove has been recycled twice by now. They tore down that first apartment you lived in, and you've never noticed a former-employee reunion for your old job posted on Facebook. Those firsts had their day, but thankfully a much better second took their place. So also God has this pattern biblically and in our lives. Be patient with the firsts, see the value that they might have, and have faith that the second that follows is the one that counts.

"I'M BUT A STRANGER HERE"

Now we live in the first, but the second is coming. While many hymns express this truth, "I'm But a Stranger Here" (*LSB* 748) by Thomas R. Taylor does this with reassuring directness. Stanza 1 contrasts our difficult life versus the simple promise of heaven to come:

> I'm but a stranger here,
>> Heav'n is my home;
> Earth is a desert drear,
>> Heav'n is my home.
> Danger and sorrow stand
> Round me on ev'ry hand;
> Heav'n is my fatherland,
>> Heav'n is my home.

Notice that the hymn describes the barren life we have here but cannot fully describe the differences we'll find in heaven. It is enough to know that the first, our dangers here, will be eclipsed in heaven. The contrast of this world versus heaven comes also in the images of storm and winter in stanza 2:

> What though the tempest rage,
>> Heav'n is my home;
> Short is my pilgrimage,
>> Heav'n is my home;
> And time's wild wintry blast
> Soon will be overpast;
> I shall reach home at last,
>> Heav'n is my home.

We don't need to know the weather in heaven or have a five-millennia forecast from there. It is enough to know that this first long winter will be over. The second, the spring of eternal life, will come, and that will be our home.

DISCUSSION QUESTIONS

1. The chapter begins by remembering the first car, apartment, or job that you had, one that wasn't very good but the second was much better. What was your experience with a bad first car, apartment, or job? How was the second much better?

2. The chapter had several examples of the first/second sequence. Which of these was most familiar and expected for you? Which of these was a new example for you of this first/second sequence?

3. One aspect of the first/second sequence is the love of repetition, the need to say the same thing twice. This is a common biblical pattern, often seen in the Psalms for example. Why does God need to repeat His larger message and actions for us to understand? For example, why were there two temples leading to Jesus, the greatest temple? Why was there a second giving of the Law in Deuteronomy when it had already been stated in Exodus?

4. The chapter described at length two prime examples of the first/second sequence in Joshua and David. Joshua had to take over for Moses in a challenging way. When have you had to start a new job, taking over for someone who was experienced and successful? How was it especially challenging for Joshua to take over for Moses?

5. David had to surpass Saul, whose work as first king was not a stellar success. Yet David had to wait, despite being already anointed. How did this patience serve David well in dealing with Saul? Also, how would more patience have helped David in other times of his life?

6. The chapter discussed Martha and Mary as an example of the first and second choice. When have you been naturally a Martha, making what seemed a good, busy choice? When do you succeed in being Mary, making a quieter, more receptive choice?

7. One of the final examples was Jairus in Mark 5 and his need for Jesus to heal his dying daughter. He had to wait, however, for the healing given first to the woman in the crowd. How easily he could have complained, "But I was first!" When have you had the same complaint when things seem to be out of sequence? What is God teaching you about patience and the first/second sequence through that experience?

CHAPTER 4

One Stands in Place of Us All

It happened in fourth grade. I was hit in the back of the head with a rock. It wasn't my fault, honest. I was minding my own business when Ross hit me in the back of the head with a rock. I think I can still feel it.

Now, remember how fourth grade works. Someone on the playground had just gotten hit in the head with a rock. Did the teacher see who threw the rock? Of course not. But did she hear the shout of the one who was hit? Instantly. So she asked the whole class of thirty the classic teacher-on-the-playground question: "Who threw the rock?" Do fourth-grade rock-throwers ever volunteer their guilt? Never, even though we all knew Ross did it.

So what happened next? Something had to happen. We had just started our thirty-minute recess. Well, that was over. Were we going inside for milk, cookies, and a story? No chance. We were going in either to put our heads down on the desk or, worse by far, we were going in for more work. Remember how on good days you had to do only the even- or the odd-numbered questions in the math book? What about that day in my fourth-grade class? Right, we lost recess and had to do all the math questions, even and odd.

How did we all feel about Ross right then? Not good. We had as much righteous wrath against him as a fourth grader can have. It wasn't fair! We didn't throw the rock, but we were the ones who had to pay.

Now, let's fast forward to an imaginary story. (I really did get hit in the head by a rock in fourth grade.) Imagine my same class as high school seniors, and imagine that Ross was on the track and field team. In fact, he was the star at shot put. He was going to the state competition for shot put, the first one ever to go from our little high school. The afternoon before he went to state, what would we have in the gym? Pep rally, of course. What about class? Canceled for the whole high school. And what class did we get out of? Math, naturally, if there's any justice in the world, and a really hard class like AP calculus. How would we have felt about Ross then? We would love Ross! He'd be the best!

THIS IS GOD'S WORST AND BEST IDEA

None of our seven principles has such a swing of emotion and application as this one. This will either cast us down to hell or lift us up to heaven. This is our death sentence or life without end. We will either complain bitterly that it isn't fair, or we will be only too happy to take the consequences and ask no questions. While our other principles so far have had a two-sided aspect of perfection/patience and first/second, this principle makes only one statement that then has these two reactions. One stands in place of us all. That's either the worst news we could hear or the best beyond imagining.

This contrast fits easily with our balance between patience and perfection. The truth that one stands in place of us all has an instant perfection to it. The deed is done, the judgment is made, and there is nothing left to say or do. Of course, this depends on our agreement with the judgment and the one who takes our place. But even when we agree with the judgment, there is also a great measure of patience needed. The judgment may be said, but the result is still largely hidden. We may be declared innocent, but we feel that we are still in the courtroom and our accusers are still shouting. So it takes patience to trust that this verdict and substitution are true and will hold over time.

> That's either the worst news we could hear or the best beyond imagining.

Again!

We have just returned from three days with our granddaughter Gabriella, who is absolutely the cutest grandchild ever. She is sixteen months old, truly never stops moving, and uses a combination of almost-word sounds and hand signals. I like her pronunciation now because whatever she is saying, I can hear it as something like, "Grandpa, you're the best!" No one else seems to hear it that way, but Gabriella and I have a special understanding. But one thing does come out clearly, "Again." When you've done something right, like reading the numbers book that she likes, once is not enough. "Again" comes through perfectly clear.

We are all a bit like Gabriella. We love "again." As we begin to study this principle, we likely resist its essential "one and done" idea because we are "again" people at heart. We want to have another chance at what we're supposed to do. We want to do it one more time. It's like when you have to put that decal on your car's license plate, the one with the new year's number. At least in Wisconsin, that little decal sticks instantly to whatever it first touches. Put it on a little crooked and think that you can just nudge it over and try again? Not a chance. For the next year, your decal is a crooked witness to two things: you should have planned this better and, boy, do these things ever stick.

But this principle says one stands in place of us all and one stands in place of all the future attempts and promises that we might make. The foundation of this is Adam, as you likely expected. The single sin of Adam and Eve was the one sin that stood for us all in the judgment of God. Romans 5 makes this clear: "Therefore, just as sin came into the world through one man, and death through sin, and so death spread to all men because all sinned" (5:12) and "For the judgment following one trespass brought condemnation" (5:16). These verses make it clear that the sin of Genesis 3 cast us all out of the garden, and there will be no return past the angel with the flaming sword (Genesis 3:24). We can argue that it isn't fair, that we have never had the chance to live in paradise, and that we would almost certainly have lasted longer than Adam and Eve. It doesn't matter. The divine principle is set. Adam stands for us all, and one sin sets the pattern of sin without escape for us all. As we study this principle, we'll have to start with that pattern of Adam and those moments in which the missteps of one become the journey for all.

THAT ONE COUNTED

People can say a thousand words, but only five will be remembered. When we interview people for a job, they will talk for an hour, but the hiring committee's discussion later will often focus on one or two sentences. The person being interviewed likely has no idea that out of all those words, these few are the ones that matter. We can be in the midst of a beautiful scene, but one thing can spoil it. (I'm once again writing at the park next to the river on a perfect summer day, but there's a crow. He's just behind me and won't stop cawing. The river sparkles, the breeze is perfect, but that crow, that crow, that nagging crow, it just won't stop.) Everything can be right, but one thing will undo it.

So this principle focuses on single words and acts. We have the foundation laid already with Adam's sin, but we can see this principle at work with other biblical moments. One act or a single word, and the judgment comes. We might be in awe that such judgment comes, but it prepares us also for the freedom from judgment that comes by one man's act.

> The missteps of one become the journey for all.

Moses is one of the best examples. We have an extensive history of Moses' exemplary life through Exodus to Deuteronomy. As we noted in the previous chapter, Moses was a man to whom God spoke as a man speaks to his friend (Exodus 33:11). What a relationship! But one act changed Moses' future. When water was needed, God told him to speak to the rock so water would flow. But instead Moses struck the rock twice. Why? Perhaps he wanted to contribute some action of his own. But this action brought immediate response as God said, "Because you did not believe in Me, to uphold Me as holy in the eyes of the people of Israel, therefore you shall not bring this assembly into the land that I have given them" (Numbers 20:12). We may be astonished at this, but Moses did not protest. The single act stood opposite all that he had done. The way to the Promised Land was barred.

That single action of Moses was enough. For another pair, it was a single act and then a single word that accompanied their action that undid them. Ananias and Sapphira were a part of the Early Christian Church in Acts 5. They sold a piece of property and brought a part of the proceeds to the apostles. Others brought the whole amount of their similar sales to the apostles (Acts 4:36–37). Ananias, however, wanted both the credit and the cash. He wanted the praise for his apparent generosity while still clutching the money to his heart. Peter confronted Ananias and asked, "Why is it that you have contrived this deed in your heart? You have not lied to men but to God" (Acts 5:4). Ananias died on the spot. When he was carried out, Sapphira came, and Peter asked if the amount brought was the price of the sale. She said it was, and Peter told her that those who carried out her husband would carry her out also. She died immediately too. One act, one rebellious sentence, and they both died. It might be noted that this was the first rebellious sin among the Early Church in Acts, an interesting parallel to the initial sin of Adam and Eve. (See *The Lutheran Study Bible* [St. Louis: Concordia Publishing House, 2009], 1842.) Adam and Eve were warned that the day they ate of the tree, they would die. Spiritually, there was an immediate death, and ultimately death entered the world. For Ananias and Sapphira, their sin brought about an immediate, physical death.

Ananias and Sapphira shared their sin and also the sudden judgment. In another instance, there is a shared role of being one in the place of all. It is not a single individual but a body of ten who would stand for the whole city of Sodom and Gomorrah, either by their presence to save or by their absence to condemn. God had determined to destroy these two cities and warned Abraham of this (Genesis 18:20–21). Abraham asked God to spare the city of Sodom if fifty righteous people could be found. God agreed and then allowed Abraham to plead down the number to ten. If ten righteous men could be found, the city would be spared (Genesis 18:32). Sadly, those ten could not be found, and for the want of those ten the whole city was destroyed. If that small number had been there, they would have stood in place of all for the saving of the city.

A good king could have also saved many people. Saul had the promise of being that king at first. But his single headstrong act of offering the sacrifice without Samuel doomed his kingship. He was told to wait seven days for Samuel to offer the sacrifice. Finally, the seventh day came, but Samuel did not. Frustrated, Saul overstepped his role and offered the sacrifice. Then Samuel arrived and announced the judgment: "But now your kingdom shall not continue. The LORD has sought out a man after His own heart, and the LORD has commanded him to be prince over His people, because you have not kept what the LORD commanded you" (1 Samuel 13:14). It was an eternal difference captured in one day by a single act. If Saul had kept this command, God's promise was that his kingdom would have lasted forever (1 Samuel 13:13). But this single act stood in place of all that might have come and was the barrier that closed Saul's kingdom.

Notice that the judgment that comes with each of these is a final judgment. There is no credit for time served and no promise of rehabilitation. We hope that a prison term would teach someone a lesson and that, upon being set free, the former prisoner would be reformed. But judgment comes upon these examples

> It was an eternal difference captured in one day by a single act.

of one sin, and that judgment promises no change, no parole, and no shortened sentence. There is no hope that good behavior will change the Judge's mind. The one act stands for all.

In fact, that judgment in the case of Adam's sin only increased our sin. Romans 5 shows that the one sin carried through in practice to all. "Therefore, just as sin came into the world through one man, and death through sin, and so death spread to all men because all sinned" (5:12). Here we have the infectious power of the one act when it is sin. Not only does the one sin bring the judgment of God, but this one sin triggers us to keep following sin.

It is like the day in fourth grade recess. One rock caused us all to lose our recess and do all the math problems. But what if that one person who threw the rock had caused us all suddenly to pick up rocks and start to throw them? That would be extreme, something happening only in a movie. But that is what happened with this single sin. We were not only trapped in it but we were trained by it for the rest of our lives. As much as we may rail against a perceived injustice, our daily, lively sin confirms that we are truly in the line of Adam and Eve. We may claim that we wouldn't have done their sin, but our sins are still daily done.

Doesn't Anyone Have the Answer?

That is the burden of this principle, the judgment against sin begun by another but carried on by ourselves. Argue as we may that our sins are not as bad as others or that we have never actually killed someone, the judgment still stands. Because one has sinned, so also all have sinned. But that is only half of this principle. More common in the Bible is the positive half of this rule. One stands in the place of us all to save us.

In the beginning of our chapter, we imagined the pep rally on the day before Ross went to the state track meet. It's a nice idea, but that's a once-a-year moment of freedom at best. But our principle of "One Stands in Place of Us All" worked every day in school. Let's go back to that high school AP calculus class. It's brutal. The homework leaves everyone asking, "Did you get any of this?" The worst is when the teacher asks for someone to go up on the board and work out the problem. No one moves. Angrily, the teacher asks, "Didn't anyone get this? Didn't anyone do the work?" Our only hope is Jessica, the math genius among us. If only she would put up her hand, go to the board, and work it out. And then she does. We hold our breath, but we don't need to. Jessica always gets it right. None of us dare to walk up with her, and nothing remotely like her answer is on our worksheets. It doesn't matter. Jessica saves us.

Our principle isn't stated by the teacher exactly, but it works out. Twenty-nine of us have no clue how to do this problem, but if Jessica can do it, then we can nod our heads, and the class can move on. The teacher might even ask, "Did you all get this? Do you see how to do this?" We all nod our heads. "Sure. Got it. Clear as a bell." The teacher might not be happy, but the principle works. Jessica goes to the board alone. One stands in the place of us all.

That's the parallel to one of the best biblical examples of our principle, a moment when the people were in desperate shape and the one who stated the principle seemed to look more for their destruction than salvation. Goliath was that man. Goliath stated our principle perfectly and seemed to embody it. Remember Goliath's challenge to the army of Israel? "Choose a man for yourselves, and let him come down to me. If he is able to fight with me and kill me, then we will be your servants. But if I prevail against him and kill him, then you shall be our servants and serve us" (1 Samuel 17:8–9). This was a perfect statement of the two-sided nature of this principle. One may stand for us all, but the outcome could go either way. As dangerous as this challenge is when you are facing a Goliath, the appeal of letting someone else do the fighting is inescapable. If only we had a giant to match theirs.

David's arrival and his complete contrast from Goliath will be a key part of the coming chapter on greatness. But we know that David fulfilled the role of "One Stands in Place of Us All." He stepped forward, as Saul the king should have, and did so without the armor of Saul. Interestingly, the Philistines, once they saw Goliath's death, did not follow through on his stated agreement that they would become Israel's slaves. The Philistines fled and were pursued, still enemies and far from being obedient slaves (1 Samuel 17:52–53). But before the battle, both sides agreed that our principle was fair. One should stand in place of us all.

A Single, Shimmering Thread

Your button is hanging on by a single thread. How'd this happen? When did all the other threads give up? You just noticed that you have only a single thread holding this button on. And it's not a button that's safely hidden, that one on the bottom of the shirt that is tucked in anyway. No, that button will never fall off. This is the middle-of-the-shirt button that, if lost, everyone will notice. And it's not that you're on your way home. No, you notice this just before the interview or the presentation you have to make. Carrying a handy sewing kit with you? Not a chance. Got a sweater you can throw on over? No, it's the dead heat of summer. It's just you and that button hanging by a single thread.

That's our principle at work. I hope you made it through the next hour of the interview and the button held. Strange how life can come down to something so small. But that's our principle of "One Stands in Place of Us All." It's much like the work of the king, as we saw with David. The work of the king in place of us all makes sense. After all, why should he live in a palace if there isn't a job to do? All that luxury has to come at a price. Another palace-dweller who embodied our principle was Queen Esther. She battled for the life of the people of Israel in a much different setting and manner than David did, but the stakes were again life and death for her and for all those watching. Think of Esther as the single, silken thread that held the lives of Israel.

Actually, the story of Esther demonstrates our principle in both its condemning and saving aspects. Haman, the king of Persia's advisor, hated a Jewish man named Mordecai, Esther's cousin. Because of his hatred, Haman planned to destroy all the people of Israel in the kingdom. Certainly greed and power were key factors in the plot, but the trigger appeared to be Mordecai's refusal to bow down to Haman at the city gate. Therefore, Haman decided all the Jews must die because of this one man (Esther 3:5–6). What a reversal this is from the role of the first Adam. The originally innocent Adam by one sin brought sin and death to all. Now Mordecai by one defiant moment, which appeared to be no sin at all, brought threatened death to all the Jews.

When the edict came that all the Jews must die, Esther appeared safe since she was the queen. No one knew she was a Jew. But Mordecai came to her and made her role clear: "Do not think to yourself that in the king's palace you will escape any more than all the other Jews. . . . Who knows whether you have not come to the kingdom for such a time as this?" (Esther 4:13–14). Esther fasted and prayed for three days, entered the king's presence boldly, and invited him and Haman to two banquets. At the end of the second meal, Esther denounced Haman and uncovered his plot to kill her and her people. The king canceled the edict of destruction and hanged Haman on the gallows Haman had prepared for Mordecai. One courageous queen, a shimmering thread of silk, stood in the place of all.

> The single, silken thread that held the lives of Israel.

There's Only One Answer

Maybe the reason math and I don't get along is that there's generally only one correct answer for a math problem. When the teacher asked, "Danny, what's the answer?" she wanted one number. My suggestion of all numbers from zero to infinity wasn't going to work. It's just one number.

So it is also with our principle. Just as the king or queen stands in place of all, so the answer that one gives must stand in place of all others. Many biblical people were called to make a stand and declare a single answer. It may or may not have been accepted, but they had to settle on a single choice.

This is often the role of the prophet. The prophetic role, much like that of the king, stands in the place of all. Prophets—like Elijah and Elisha or anyone who speaks God's Word—stand in place of us all by speaking the one thing we need to hear. Joshua filled that role in the end of his life as he challenged Israel to decide their allegiance to God or others. He gave them options and then a single example in himself: "Choose this day whom you will serve, whether the gods your fathers served in the region beyond the River, or the gods of the

One courageous queen, a shimmering thread of silk.

Amorites in whose land you dwell. But as for me and my house, we will serve the LORD" (Joshua 24:15). The people affirmed they would serve the true God, so Joshua set a stone of witness to their choice (Joshua 24:27). As Moses presented the Law on two tablets of stone, so Joshua ended his leadership of Israel by establishing the stone of witness to recall Israel's vow to follow God.

When Joshua challenged Israel, they followed. One spoke for all, and soon the one was joined by the many. But for another prophet, the result was the exact opposite. Elijah stood alone against the 450 prophets of Baal (1 Kings 18). Elijah gave a challenge similar to Joshua's, contrasting Baal with the true God and asking if the people would continue to limp between two opinions (1 Kings 18:21). However, opposite of Joshua's challenge, Elijah was met with silence. He then stated the essence of our principle: "I, even I only, am left a prophet of the LORD, but Baal's prophets are 450 men" (1 Kings 18:22). One alone stood for the true God, and he would continue to stand alone through the day's challenge of calling down fire from heaven.

But even after the complete success of defeating the prophets of Baal and seeing heavenly fire consume his sacrifice, Elijah still saw himself as the only one left. After Queen Jezebel threatened to kill him, Elijah fled to the desert. After forty days in the desert, God came to him and Elijah repeated his view that he was the only faithful one left (1 Kings 19:10). God had an interesting balance to that claim. He sent Elijah back to the work that needed his hand alone, the anointing of kings and prophets. For that, yes, Elijah was the one, the only one, to do the work. But God also reminded Elijah that he was far from being the only one to believe, as there were seven thousand left in Israel who were faithful still to Him (1 Kings 19:15–18).

That readiness to serve, to say the words that others couldn't say, continues also to the New Testament, especially with the disciples of Jesus. They ask the questions that we want to ask, such as the meaning of parables (Mark 4:10) and the meaning of Jesus' more challenging words (John 14:5, 8). But they also give a witness that no one else dares. The best example might be Peter's confession in Matthew 16 when Jesus asked who men said that He was and then challenged the Twelve by asking who they thought He was. Peter spoke for us all for all time when he answered, "You are the Christ, the Son of the living God" (Matthew 16:16). Peter's confession echoes to this day.

The scene of the two men at Jesus' crucifixion continues that action of speaking for us all. The repentant thief on the cross recognized Jesus as the merciful, returning king and asked to be remembered graciously. His bold insights stand for us all, and we're glad to join him when Jesus said, "Truly, I say to you, today you will be with Me in paradise" (Luke 23:43). This man's confession balanced the insight by the centurion upon Jesus' death. In Mark 15, we hear the centurion in charge of Jesus' death say, "Truly this man was the Son of God" (Mark 15:39). In the darkness of Good Friday, the centurion and the thief could see the gracious King and Son of God. Matching their question in another time of deathly darkness is the Philippian jailer who was about to kill himself when the prison doors miraculously sprang open. But Paul stopped him, and the man asked the question for all time, "Sirs, what must I do to be saved?" (Acts 16:30). Paul gave the answer with equal brevity and certainty: "Believe in the Lord Jesus, and you will be saved" (Acts 16:31). These three men bring out three crucial sentences in the midst of darkness and death, giving timeless words for all Christians in their most difficult days.

I'll Ask Him

Did you have it worked out in your family who did the asking? Someone had to ask Mom or Dad if you could go swimming, have dessert first, or get a puppy. You plotted this out carefully. Who's going to ask, where, and when? Find just the right moment, look for the signs that Dad's in a good mood, and then ask. You even had the words worked out in advance. Start casually with "Uhh, Dad, uhh, we were wondering . . ." But beyond the words, it all hinged on who would do the asking.

The priest was that person, the one to do the asking. We see that role carried out in the tent of meeting, the tabernacle, and the temple. We see it also done when one dares to stand alone, bearing the guilt that wasn't even their own. We put our whole relationship and hope in that person's actions. We have already seen this willingness to stand before God alone in Moses as he met God in the tent of meeting. We will see this same bold action in several others, both in the formal setting and sense of a priest and also in those outside that formal designation. This is perhaps the most dramatic example of our principle when someone volunteers to face God and says, "I'll ask Him."

The priests were set apart in clothing and preparation to stand alone before God. Exodus 29 gives the extensive directions for Aaron and his sons to be the priests in the tabernacle. Their clothing, the offerings they brought, and the sprinkling of the blood upon them to consecrate them—all these set them apart from all other people. The priests' continued service over hundreds of years in the tabernacle and the two temples demonstrates our principle of one for all. However, to serve God carried serious dangers. For example, Leviticus 10 records the death of Nadab and Abihu, the sons of Aaron, consumed by fire when they offered unauthorized fire before God. Let's have someone else stand in place of us all when God's fire bursts out.

Besides the fiery threat, the priests had other challenging roles that put them first in front of all others. The priests carried the ark of the covenant into the flooding waters of the Jordan River while all of Israel watched and waited (Joshua 3). Nothing happened until their feet touched the water, and then the waters divided so they could walk through. We can imagine that the people gladly let the priests go first and divide the waters for the sake of all others.

The priests stepped forward to face not only raging waters but their sins and the sins of the people. In offering sacrifices on the Day of Atonement, Aaron was to begin first by presenting a bull as an offering for himself and to make atonement for his house (Leviticus 16:11). Then he would be able to make atonement for the Holy Place (Leviticus 16:16), and finally he would make atonement for the sins of the people (Leviticus 16:21). In the place of all, he faced the threefold guilt of himself, the Holy Place, and all the people. During it all, the people of Israel could watch in hushed awe and thankful reception.

We might broaden the role of bearing the sins of others a bit to include those who were not a part of the priesthood. Abigail took that dangerous role when she confronted David as he raced toward her home, ready to kill her foolish husband and those in his camp. Abigail was entirely innocent of Nabal's foolish confrontation with David, but she instead put the guilt upon herself when she met David, saying, "On me alone, my lord, be the guilt" (1 Samuel 25:24). How easy it would have been for her to blame all on Nabal and to escape the destruction alone. But she stood in the place of all, daring to stop David by her gracious words. Death was about to wash over her people. Only by letting the anger break upon her could she save them all.

ONCE IS ENOUGH

You can see our principle going down the highway at the end of most any summer weekend. Think about the line of campers, trailers, and RVs heading back into town. The bikes, the kayaks, and the overstuffed luggage holders are all teetering on top of the load. The back windows are blocked with sleeping bags, pillows, and the odd axe handle. In the back seat, children are heads down, either asleep or working their phones now that they are finally back in civilization. In the front, Mom and Dad are talking a little, reassuring each other that it was a good trip and it was worth going. But one thing everyone will agree to: we do this trip once a summer, and once is enough.

Maybe other trips, events, or sports have the same finality. But the summer camping trip especially works this way. Go once a year and that's enough. You can say you are campers, real stayed-out-in-the-rain tent campers. But that one Friday-Saturday-Sunday is enough for the year. So also remarkably the single weekend of Good Friday to Easter stands for all year and all eternity. That one three-day journey of one man, Jesus, fills the need for all of us for all time. And while He must bear the burden, pain, and darkness of death, we need only to read, understand, and believe. Then His journey over His three days is more than enough for us.

THE ULTIMATE ONE IN PLACE OF US ALL

Throughout these many examples, you have likely been hearing echoes of the greater work done by Jesus as the One in place of all. We can see Him serving as prophet, priest, and king along with parallels to many of the others we have noted. Yet beyond their actions, Jesus uniquely stands in place of us as the new Adam. He is the One by whose wounds we are healed, the One for whom the heavens opened and whom the Father acknowledged as His beloved Son.

Jesus' role as the One in place of all takes us back to Adam. Remember our image of children choosing someone in the family to go to Dad or Mom? The youngest ones know they don't have a chance of getting Dad to say yes to a puppy. So they wait until their oldest brother comes home from college. He's the one to ask Dad! So he does, but what if Dad's response is "You kids are always asking and promising. But how does it turn out? You promised to take care of the goldfish. Remember that?" (Dad points to the cracked and empty aquarium.) Dad could go on, pointing to the other broken promises—the piano that is never played, though someone said they had to have it. But the older brother never made and broke those promises. He cared for his guinea pig perfectly. He actually took out the recycling every Friday, and he never forgot his turn to do the dishes.

Death was about to wash over her people.

What's he going to say when all the failures are brought out? The older brother is silent and lets the memories of every broken promise wash over him as though he's done the breaking. His perfection is not a barrier to this but is the only way for all the sins of his siblings to find a single place to go. So it is with Christ. We will discuss more of this in our final theme, "Perfection Welcomes Failure," but we see it already in action here with "One Stands in Place of Us All." Only His perfection lets Him be the silent, suffering Lamb (Isaiah 53:5–7).

This perfection and yet willingness to be the one standing in place of our failure is a perfect balance of perfection and patience. Jesus' willingness to be accounted as the complete sinner is the strangest perfection. And only perfect patience would endure the taunts and tears of the cross without a defending word. Only His perfect trust in the Father allowed Him to put Himself into the Father's hands and wait the three days of the tomb.

This perfection/patience balance is what makes Jesus as the new Adam remarkable. God redeems the world by sending His

Son in the model of Adam. And yet it is only after thousands of years that He comes. And He comes with important differences from the role and work of Adam. We noted Adam's work earlier in Romans 5, whereby his sin led to the sin and death of all. We received both his practice and penalty. But the new Adam of Christ in place of us all gives us life despite our continued sin. We might have expected that Jesus as the new Adam would come as a groundbreaking example of holy living. He could destroy the barrier of sin and then turn to us, saying, "There, that's how it's done. Now get busy." But then His victory would only be our defeat. His example would crush us as an impossible load.

But the new Adam does not bring a repeated pattern of failure as did the first Adam. Instead, He gives us the full measure of His own success. "For as by the one man's disobedience the many were made sinners, so by the one man's obedience the many will be made righteous" (Romans 5:19). This righteousness is not made of second chances and trying harder. God has seen through all our promises. But we need only this One, whose perfection brings His gifts to us. As with the family mentioned earlier, if the older brother asks for the puppy, then it is given because he, the elder brother alone, has kept all his promises. So it is with Christ, our Brother.

A Little Boy's Worries—A Father's Work

On the farm when I was growing up, the biggest job of harvest season was combining the oats. For a week, we harvested oats with only a small window of time to get it done. One year when I was about twelve, the combine burned out an important bearing, stopping the machine. We went to the International Harvester dealer and got a new bearing. But it didn't fit, being too big in diameter to slip into the bearing housing. The dealer insisted it was correct, and it was the only one he had.

What to do? I went to sleep worrying and woke up at 5:00 a.m. just as anxious. I went down to Mom in the kitchen. I told her that I didn't know what we were going to do about that bearing. Mom was surprised that I was worried. She said, "Oh, Dad got up at 3:00 and fixed it." I was amazed. I went to the barn, and Dad said that he simply sanded the outside diameter of the bearing with emery cloth, a metal-cutting sandpaper, until it fit. How long? Dad guessed about an hour. For him, it was no big deal, but for me, it confirmed that boyhood feeling that Dad could fix anything. We combined that day and through to the end of the season with no problems.

One quiet man's work, hidden from us all and done with ease, leaves us amazed, like I was amazed by Dad and we are amazed at God's work. In the Father's accounting, all has been done already. When we weren't watching, He quietly did all the work we had left undone. He mercifully paid the bill we had accumulated, stepped out on the journey to the cross, and gave up His last breath. He didn't stop in mid-act to ask, "Did you see that? Wasn't that something?" He only gave the benefits to us with the gracious power of God redeeming His children.

> One quiet man's work, hidden from us all and done with ease, leaves us amazed.

TRUSTING THE GLUE

If I had known that Dad was going to get up at 3:00 to fix the combine, I would have slept much better that night. Of course that would have taken faith. That's the greatest challenge of the "One Stands in Place of Us All" theme. Much of the principle is unseen, and we have no way to test it now.

It's like gluing a joint in woodworking. When you put a joint together, like the mortise and tenon joint that holds together chair legs or the sides of a table, the glue is all that holds the piece together. It's also completely hidden. You fit the joint together without glue and feel that it's snug. But once you put the glue on and clamp the joint together, it's time to trust. The joint and the glue are completely hidden. And taking it apart to see if it's working ruins the glue. It takes at least an hour for common wood glue to set. So trust and wait.

Isn't that the balance needed with this principle? The work of Christ in our place is perfect. He said, "It is finished," and the temple curtain was torn open (John 19:30; Luke 23:45). However, this perfection is largely hidden from us. We can't ascend to heaven to check if the thief on the cross is there. We can't go into Jesus' Easter-morning tomb to see the moment of the resurrection. We cannot fast forward to our own resurrection and verify the transformation of our bodies. There is a perfect union in Christ of human and divine. But that union, which promises to take the entire load of our sins, can only be trusted. Skeptically test it, and it's ruined. Trust that the Carpenter has done His work.

So in the end, I think I can still feel where I got hit in the head by that rock. And recess being turned into extra math was not fair. But this principle is more than a schoolyard injustice. Biblically, we have a wealth of examples of those who stood in place of us all. We can admire and even follow for a few steps the courage and graciousness of David and Abigail, and perhaps recognize a moment when we alone have the word that needs to be said. But thank goodness, this principle is really about Him, the new Adam. He alone stands for us in a sinful state we can't bear to watch. He alone rises from the dead with the promise of opening our tombs also. He is the Triumphant One who stands with and for us all.

"MY HOPE IS BUILT ON NOTHING LESS"

Many hymns celebrate the completeness of Jesus' sacrifice alone. The hymn "My Hope Is Built on Nothing Less" (*LSB* 575) by Edward Mote focuses on the rock of Jesus' work in contrast to the disappearing sand of our own work. This imagery recalls especially the ending of the Sermon on the Mount, where Jesus contrasts those who build their lives on the rock of His Word, which withstands all storms, versus those who build on sand, quickly washed away (Matthew 7:24–27). Two stanzas in particular stand out, stanzas 1 and 3 with the repeated refrain:

> My hope is built on nothing less
>
> Than Jesus' blood and righteousness;
>
> No merit of my own I claim
>
> But wholly lean on Jesus' name.
>
> On Christ, the solid rock, I stand;
>
> All other ground is sinking sand.

> His oath, His covenant and blood
>
> Support me in the raging flood;
>
> When ev'ry earthly prop gives way,
>
> He then is all my hope and stay.
>
> On Christ, the solid rock, I stand;
>
> All other ground is sinking sand.

What a picture of trust this hymn brings. The storm rages, but within that storm, His calm Word speaks more clearly. The waves race toward us, but His blood remains. His blood is never washed away but is always the high tide mark of God's single sacrifice. We have only this one hope and stay, one anchor, but that one is enough for us all.

DISCUSSION QUESTIONS

1. The chapter began with the story of one person being hit with a rock leading to the end of recess and more math. When have you experienced the same sort of injustice, one person's wrong affecting everyone else? How have you and others reacted to this?

2. On the other hand, the chapter told the fictitious story of Ross going to state track and the whole school getting out of math. When have you had this unexpected benefit from someone else's accomplishment?

3. The chapter noted several biblical people who showed exceptional courage when stepping forward in place of others. Take at least one of these that were mentioned: David, Abigail, Esther, or the priests facing the Jordan River. How did they do it, going forward when all others were retreating?

4. Continuing from the previous question, to what extent are we expected to share the courage of David and Esther?

5. The chapter highlighted the role of Jesus as the new Adam as described in Romans 5 and 1 Corinthians 15. God is determined to save the world through the model and role of Adam, despite Adam's sin. Why would God persist in this role of Adam, one in place of all?

6. The principle promises Jesus as the perfect One in our place. However, how does this promise at this time stretch our patience and faith?

7. In the sidebar, I described the camping trip, three days of rain in a tent, and that it was more than enough for a year. When have you had this sort of once-is-enough experience? How is it remarkable that Jesus subjects Himself to the ultimate once-is-enough weekend for the saving of the world?

CHAPTER 5

Grace Upends Our World

We picked rocks every spring on the farm. For a week, my parents, my sister, and I walked through the fields, picking up the rocks too big to ignore for another year. It was simple, dull work. Pick up the rock. Put it in a wire basket. Carry the basket to the wagon and dump it out. Repeat. For a week. My mother said that if, after five minutes, there was anything about picking rocks that either amused you or confused you, there was something wrong with you.

The only time that the job was even barely exciting was when we had a big rock, one we had been skating over for years. But finally the frost would push it up too high to be ignored. Then Dad and I would bring a stone boat next to the rock because it was much too large to be picked up and lifted onto the wagon. A stone boat is a flat bed of boards about three feet wide and seven feet long that is dragged on the ground behind a tractor. Lift up the rock with six-foot-long crowbars made from old Model T axles. Work your way around it, prying little by little until you get the rock out of the hole and flipped onto the stone boat.

Simple. But there was one problem. The rock didn't want to move. You could tell it about its new home with the other rocks in the gully behind the barn. You could promise it new friends and exciting adventures. Tell it anything you want. (After a week of picking rocks, you're starting to talk to the rocks. My mother is worrying about you.) But while you're prying that rock up, if that crowbar slips just once, where is that rock going to go? Right back into the hole. All the promises in the world won't draw it out of its hole.

We're these rocks. God's grace comes to biblical people and to us with wonderful promises. God promises to take us to a new home, His own, and to lift us up literally from the deepest rut, our graves. He promises to give us new people by the millions for eternity. Those promises also came very specifically to many biblical people as they were lifted up to be the leaders for the people of Israel and later the Christian Church. They were assured that God would be with them and that all they would need would be provided. The former oppression under which they lived would be done, and a new freedom would come.

But we're rocks. Often we respond to grace by falling into the same rut we've been in. We even complain that our comfortable spot has now been disturbed. We either flat-out deny the possibility of God's promises being true or we do all we can to defeat them. Then when our own hands cause us to slip, we complain that God hasn't done enough.

It is a wonder that God even bothers to give His grace. Yet He does because, despite our objections, He brings us to the promises He has made. He turns Jonah around and brings him to Nineveh. He stiffens Gideon's backbone, answers his questions, and calms his doubts. He makes the murdering Pharisee Saul into the greatest missionary of the first century. Through Paul's preaching, He turned the world upside down. And His grace upends our world still today.

THIS TIME, IT'S ABOUT ME

This theme is more about us than we've seen so far. This theme balances our previous one, "One Stands in Place of Us All," which put us into the background while another stood up for us entirely alone. We were the crowd watching David battle Goliath for us. Esther alone saved the people of Israel. But now it's time to swing the pendulum the other way and focus a bit more on our role as the promises of God's grace turn our world upside down.

The power is all still in God's grace since we are all unwilling rocks that can neither hear nor understand God's promises. And there's nothing we can do to bring those promises to us in the first place.

But it is that very rebellion against the promises that makes up half of this theme. First, we have to see the various ways that biblical people heard the upending promises of God's grace and how they did all they could to slip back into their ruts. They were even more rebellious than rocks for rocks are only stubborn because of gravity. But people are far more creative. They complain, question, and endlessly suggest alternatives. They even get up and go the wrong way. People are wandering rocks, looking for a better rut. As we survey these responses, we'll see ourselves and the creative ways our fallen nature resists God's direction and mercy.

But despite our rebellious reaction to grace, there is also a positive side. God raises the stubborn rocks, and their very resistance becomes a demonstration of His grace. You can't let the rocks win. When Dad and I found a rock that was just too much for us and our crowbars, we didn't give up. If crowbars won't do it, let's come out with the Farmall 300 tractor with its front-end loader. That would lift most anything. But if that rock was really serious, there was always my uncle and his D6 Caterpillar bulldozer. That D6 Cat lived to dig out any rock foolish enough to dare it. Just lean on your crowbar and enjoy the show.

> People are wandering rocks, looking for a better rut.

So we'll see God's patience at work again. We might have expected instant perfection, for God to say "Move!" and move that rock right away. We often clamor with God for that kind of instant perfection. But strangely when the grace of God announces astonishing changes, we often rebel against any instant perfection that would upend our lives. We need to see how His patient relationship with us brings about the changes He has planned. But God doesn't just endure with us in this relationship; He reminds us that, as much as we are focused on the frightening changes around us, His hand is at work on us. God wants to lift up our sight beyond what is disturbingly new to what is timelessly true. His grace comes only to save but must do so by lifting us out of our present rut and onto His means of carrying us.

ONLY IF YOU TELL ME NO

Our granddaughter Gabriella is a wonderful, active, happy girl. She is sixteen months old with, it seems, 16,000 miles of running already behind her. She is a barely-guided missile of constant motion. She was at our house this past weekend, and we loved every minute of it. But we're grandparents, so our house is not childproof anymore. You know how it is. Gabriella's house has safety latches on all the cabinet doors, there are no figurines on wobbly pedestal tables, and there is a childproof gate before the steps. We don't have any of that, and Gabriella knew it instantly. If it would make us worry, then that was the most interesting thing in the house for her. On the other hand, the steps going upstairs were wide open. She loves steps, and I was ready to go up and down all day with her. But no barrier, no interest. If the childproof gate isn't there and I'm there to help her, then it's just not worth doing.

Every parent knows how this is. There seems to be an instant misdirection placed into every child. If I can squeeze myself into a place I shouldn't be, then that's where I'm going. If I shouldn't be playing under the pine trees, then the pine needles under the trees are the most interesting thing in the world. And what we practice as children, we perfect as adults.

We find this resistance in dramatic moments throughout the Bible. The first example is the rebellious act of Adam and Eve. They had only the one directive to not eat of the tree of the knowledge of good and evil (Genesis 2:17). However simple that might be, it was the one thing to do. In a completely grace-filled world, they upended their world with this rebellion.

While this first sin began our rebellious acts, we see our theme most clearly with other biblical people who were given extraordinary opportunities and, at least at first, rebelled. Jonah is a perfect example of this. Consider the clear directions God gave him: "Go to Nineveh, that great city, and call out against it" (Jonah 1:2). Jonah had the double incentive of being called personally by God to deliver His message. And he got to give the message of impending destruction against Israel's bitter enemy. It would be a "One Stands in Place of Us All" opportunity, much like Elijah's confrontation with the 450 prophets of Baal (1 Kings 18). Jonah had the chance to see God not only upend his life but also upend the entire city of Nineveh.

But Jonah fled by ship to Tarshish, and while the exact location is debated, it was clearly in the opposite direction of Nineveh. God had to renew the call with an even more dramatic act, the rescue of Jonah from the great fish after three days. Then Jonah finally obeyed God's call, and Jonah traveled back to Nineveh.

This sequence of Jonah's call and all that followed is a pattern we can see repeated in other occurrences of this theme. The gracious call of God comes to a man or woman. Out of fear or rebellion, they pursue the opposite direction. God then intervenes, often using different means to reinforce the initial message.

> God wants to lift up our sight beyond what is disturbingly new to what is timelessly true.

There is an opportunity for the one who was called to hear the initial message again and to act upon it. People's doubting and rebellious nature is a general constant, but so is God's patience shown through His renewed reach.

This pattern of resistance might be seen especially well with the people of the exodus. Moses came, announcing his meeting with God and His plan to free Israel from four hundred years of slavery (Exodus 4:30–31). Initially, the people welcomed the good news. This is a bit like the first five minutes of rock picking, when it's new and you actually stop to look at the colors of the rocks as you pick them. But very soon it simply becomes work. The fields stretch out in front of you, and you notice that the next field to pick has even more rocks than this one. So also trouble soon began when Pharaoh heard of Moses' return and his plan. Then the people were told to make bricks without straw (Exodus 5:7–9). When this hardship came, then the leaders turned against Moses so that Moses had to cry out to God, noting that since he came, only evil had come upon the people (Exodus 5:20–23).

This conflict became the trigger for the ten plagues. God spoke through Moses by His powerful signs to turn the hearts of Israel and to compel Pharaoh to set the people free. The hardships that came with the initial promise of freedom likely had two important purposes for the people. First, the inertia of four hundred years of slavery had to be overcome. What a four-century-long rut they were in. They knew only Egypt and slavery. Freedom in their own land was a memory, likely long forgotten, and bringing it up was only painful. The inertia of slavery had to be pried up and overcome, not only by the gracious promises of deliverance from above, but by the harsh crowbars of Pharaoh's demands from below.

Also, the people not only resisted God's gracious call at the start, but they also questioned His call long down the road. Consider how Israel continued to question God as He led them through the wilderness and provided manna for their food. Before the Red Sea, they asked Moses what he had done to them by bringing them out of Egypt (Exodus 14:11–12). They later quarreled about the food and drink (Exodus 16:3; 17:3). We would hope that someone in the camp would have remembered more clearly the bitter food of slavery, the despised making of bricks, and the certainty of Egypt's increased hatred for Israel after the deaths of the firstborn and Pharaoh's army. Did anyone seriously imagine that they could return to the status quo of slavery in Egypt? No, having been pried up from their four-hundred-year rut, they couldn't settle back down just as before. The rut they had been in was filled with the sand covering the graves of the firstborn and the silt of the Red Sea washing up the remains of Pharaoh's army. Their slavery stone could never fall back into its old place.

The people of the exodus were moved by God's gracious call and reacted with repeated doubt. We might expect to see this sort of movement biblically again, and we do in the New Testament. One New Testament example repeats the most significant patterns that we saw in the exodus: important people and events, doubt, renewed miracles, and a journey both to and from Egypt.

Their slavery stone could never fall back into its old place.

The New Testament account that follows this pattern involves Joseph, engaged to Mary, in Matthew 1. Joseph and Mary were engaged when Mary conceived by the Holy Spirit and was found to be carrying the Son of God. Grace certainly upended both Mary's and Joseph's worlds!

Matthew tells us only that Mary was found to be with child from the Holy Spirit (1:18). Soon thereafter, we hear Mary's joy in the Magnificat expressed to Elizabeth (Luke 1:56), and we can only imagine how much emotion she felt. Joseph had a different reaction when he heard of Mary's pregnancy. He likely longed for the life they formerly had and the future they had planned. With dignity and kindness, he decided to divorce Mary quietly. However, this was exactly the opposite of what God intended, so God spoke to Joseph in a dream, the first of four dreams to Joseph (Matthew 1:20; 2:13, 19, 22). Having heard the message now more clearly, Joseph embraced the grace that had come to him and Mary. Joseph overcame his natural shock and fulfilled his several roles: husband to Mary, earthly father to Jesus, and a Moses-like leader of the family into and then out of Egypt so that the words of Hosea would be fulfilled: "Out of Egypt I called My son" (Hosea 11:1; Matthew 2:15).

Joseph's final movement toward God's gracious call repeated

that exodus experience in Jesus' infant life, and it also demonstrated another repeated aspect of how God's call of grace upends one's life. Here is a field for patient faith that sees all of life cast down and yet trusts that God has a purpose for what is happening. Joseph must have wondered how the worst news concerning Mary could become a blessing. God patiently spoke to him repeatedly to reassure him. Grace upended his world, and for a long, trembling moment Joseph hovered over returning to his former place or being moved to this new station as the husband to the mother of the Son of God.

Hiding behind the Couch— Leaping onto the Bed

When you first bring a pet home, how does it fit in? We lived through two extremes. Rocky was a stray cat that came into our garage one night searching for food. We fed Rocky outside for a couple weeks, but we could see he needed serious care. So we finally caught him and took him to the vet. I never knew ten pounds of terrified cat could bite, scratch, and fight like he did. The National Finals Rodeo should have it as an event: Frightened Cat Wrestling. After going to the vet, we brought Rocky home. We assured him that here he was safe and loved and would be well fed. He didn't believe it. Only after weeks, maybe months, did he begin to trust us. Eventually he came to know that he was never going to be hurt and would always be loved. In turn, he became the most loving, trusting pet we've ever had.

On the other hand, Abby the beagle was at home from day one. We went to the animal shelter and picked out Abby as our new dog because she was so quiet and timid. Other dogs barked, but Abby just looked at us with those take-me-home beagle eyes. So we took her home. And she knew she was home. After being in the house an hour, she jumped up on our three-year-old daughter's bed as Nicole was being put to sleep. She assumed this was her bed too, and it was from day one.

Our biblical examples of grace upending our world follow these two patterns. We've already seen some of the first examples, the reluctance of a Rocky. Grace comes with its promises and reassurances, but Jonah, Joseph, and even the people of Israel all had a natural caution. Rocky hid under the couch while Jonah found himself under the sea. Only with the patient coaxing of God, His repeated promises, and His strong protective hand could these frightened biblical men begin to trust that it was grace that overturned their lives.

On the other hand, we can see examples of beagle-like acceptance and joy. Abby never doubted that we were her family and our house was her home. She wasn't sure anyone else should come into the house. In fact, since we lived in the parsonage next to the church, she stood at our front window on Sundays and barked incessantly at the people going past her to church. She was a terrible church greeter. But she absolutely trusted that she was our dog and was the last dog that would ever run away from home.

This is the ready acceptance that we see with many biblical people whom God graciously called. For some, this was a grace they had sought and hoped for. For others, it was as unexpected as Rocky being taken into the house. But regardless of prior expectations, we'll see that grace can come and create an immediate trust and welcome. With that, a changed life begins.

Abby had no idea that we were coming that late afternoon to find her. I suppose she had gotten used to people coming, looking her over, and moving on. We perhaps looked no different than others, and we certainly weren't worth a bark from her. We weren't necessarily looking for a beagle, just a good dog. But adopting Abby was even more exciting because it was an unexpected meeting.

Perhaps the best example of an unexpected meeting that was embraced occurred with the apostle Paul. Certainly, his life was turned upside down by grace. Others might have been neutral to the work of God and only surprised when they were met by His gracious call. But Paul as Saul, the murdering Pharisee, was actively destroying the people of God and was knowledgeable about the claims of the Christians. On his journey to Damascus in Acts 9, he was certainly seeking Christians but never imagined he was the one being sought by Christ. When confronted by Jesus with the blinding light, Paul only asked, "Who are You, Lord?" (Acts 9:5). Jesus identified Himself and directed Paul to Damascus where he would be told what he was to do (Acts 9:6). Paul spent the following three days without food or drink praying before Ananias restored his sight (Acts 9:9, 11–12).

We can imagine that during those three days Paul asked a lot of astonished questions, a mixture of seeking direction for his life and of repenting for that which he did not know he was doing. After his sight was restored, Paul then immediately began to preach that Jesus was the Son of God to the astonishment of all. They asked, "Is not this the man who made havoc in Jerusalem of those who called upon this name?" (Acts 9:21). Paul's embrace of the Gospel went on without question for the remainder of his life. His confidence in God's work was expressed in his autobiographical words that were offered as models for all Christians: "I press on toward the goal for the prize of the upward call of God in Christ Jesus" (Philippians 3:14). By his travels, his preaching of Christ crucified, and his endurance of imprisonment and death, Paul showed the full effect of grace that upended his world.

That's My Place and I Know It

Pets know their place. Or they know how to claim a place and convince us that they're right. Abby climbed onto Nicole's bed and settled in that first night. Sleep in a wire kennel? You've got to be kidding. Abby chose Nicole's bed plus two blankets under her, nothing less. Rocky the cat slept on the top of either the living room couch or my chair, stretched out with one front leg straight ahead and the other leg hanging straight down. He looked completely exhausted. And why not? After all, he slept only eighteen hours a day. So we'd leave him be and sit somewhere else. Rocky knew his place.

So God's grace moves many, and they appear instantly to know their place. For these, God's call is immediately embraced and His mercy draws in many people. In Luke 7, we see a woman who knew her place, though it appeared as a scandalous mistake to others. The woman, defined only as a woman of the city who was a sinner, came to Jesus while He was eating at the home of Simon the Pharisee. Without invitation and certainly without encouragement from those around her, she took her place at the feet of Jesus. She wet His feet with her tears, dried them with her hair, and anointed them with perfume. Simon was aghast at her presumptuous place and actions. But Jesus told the parable of the two debtors, ending with the truth that her sins, which were many, were forgiven for she loved much (Luke 7:47). Forgiveness put her in her place, and she embraced it.

Forgiveness put her in her place, and she embraced it.

Another woman who knew her place secured by grace was the Syrophoenician woman of Mark 7. Her demonized daughter needed Jesus' healing, so she begged Him to heal her. Jesus appeared to put her off with the reminder that it was for the children of Israel that He had come. One did not take the children's bread and give it to the dogs. The woman didn't argue about her place but reminded Jesus that even the dogs ate the pieces slipped off the table. Jesus commended her for her faith, and her daughter was healed.

While we could go on further, one last woman in a place of grace was the woman caught in adultery in John 8. She didn't look for that place of judgment or expect a merciful end when she was brought before Jesus under the charge of adultery. But Jesus, who was the true target of the crowd's hatred, stood beside her in her danger and disarmed the crowd by saying that those without sin could cast the first stone (John 8:7). When all had left, He asked, "'Woman, where are they? Has no one condemned you?' She said, 'No one, Lord.' And Jesus said, 'Neither do I condemn you; go, and from now on sin no more'" (John 8:10–11). Her place of death became the place of life when grace upended her world.

In these three examples, the grace that moved these women brought them to Jesus' side. This moving grace was not a crushing blow. Much like our opening image of the rock being slid onto the stone boat, so these women were moved. God did not bury them deeper but instead moved them. (Interestingly, the woman of John 8 might certainly have been literally buried as a stone but instead was moved by grace.) Further, grace didn't elevate them to a position above others. None of them argued that they were just as good as or even better than others. The woman of Luke 7 didn't argue that her sins were no worse than those of Simon the Pharisee. Jesus didn't reveal the sins of the woman caught in adultery in order to lift her safely above others. Mercy doesn't simply raise or lower us compared to others. It slides us to a whole new place. On the farm, we didn't bury a stone deeper. Our goal was to slide it onto the stone boat and bring it to a new place.

So grace upended these lives by placing them beside Jesus. The women found a new significance and security in that place beside Him. While the gravitational pull of their past shouted that they had no reason to be there—a sinful woman in the Pharisee's house, a Syrophoenician woman asking a Jewish teacher for help—yet the grace that drew them gave them their place. There should have been no hope for the woman in John 8. We might imagine that she was flinching, waiting for the first stone to come flying. But being beside Jesus brought a new security. Surely by the end of the narrative she was looking up. She likely saw the last of the stones fall from her accusers' hands. The stones didn't fly in judgment but fell in admission of

Her place of death became the place of life when grace upended her world.

guilt. Grace moved these women beside Jesus, where they found a new status and a new safety.

NOW I SEE IT!

I was riding my motorcycle down a road that I use at least every other day. Nothing new, all the same. Wait! Since when were there apple trees there? For the first time all summer, I noticed apples, beautiful, just-turning-red apples, covering the trees along the road. I doubt that I ever really looked at these trees for the last ten or eleven months, but now, with all those apples bending down the limbs, I couldn't miss them.

You notice the same things, don't you? You miss seeing something until suddenly there it is! Think about the week when the lilacs bloom and the cherry trees blossom. All of a sudden, you see them for the first time. You know you've ignored them for months. But not anymore.

Our theme of grace upending your world allows us to see others and ourselves suddenly with new eyes. You might have ignored someone at work, not deliberately shunning them, but just going past them with your head buried in your phone. But then there was the night you discovered a flat tire on your car in the parking lot and that same person was the only one who stopped to help you change your flat. You never saw him the same again. The fruit of kindness couldn't be missed and wouldn't be forgotten. I wonder how many people are fruitful trees simply waiting for their season to come. Perhaps we might allow that grace intends to upend our perception of each believer if we would only see the fruit they're about to bear.

I Didn't Think It Was That Big

When we dug up one of the larger rocks, we knew it was bigger than we could move by hand. But as we began to dig around the rock, it got even bigger. It was always a stony iceberg waiting to be uncovered. But unlike an iceberg, we got to actually see 100 percent of the rock. Crowbar it out of that hole and flip it over onto the stone boat, and you'd be surprised at how much stone you've got.

So also when grace upends the lives of men and women, a much larger person is waiting to be seen. Grace displays a new side to the world and even to themselves. Grace upends a stone that others might have ignored, but then shows the true colors and surprising shape that was waiting underneath.

Many of our biblical examples have this 90-percent-unseen quality that waits for grace to upend it. For a man who sees grace turn his world upside down and then displays a new side, it's hard to beat Noah. When God directs Noah to build the ark because of the coming flood, we find no opposition from Noah. Unlike many key biblical people such as Moses and Jeremiah, who question God's direction and choice of themselves, Noah gets the plans and starts to build. Hearing the directions for building, it is said of Noah simply: "Noah did this; he did all that God commanded him" (Genesis 6:22).

> The stones didn't fly in judgment but fell in admission of guilt.

What an extraordinary set of commands in the context of the coming destruction of the world! Noah could have had so many questions and reasons to delay. Why are You destroying the world? Why save me? How will I ever build this? All the animals—why not just make new ones? Noah could have been a stubborn rock, buried in the rut of life as he knew it. But had he been only that, he would have been a rock thoroughly buried by the flood. Instead, he was overturned by grace and showed the world the unthinkable: an ark filled with animals that could sail over the floodwaters. And Noah and his family were transformed to become the new Adam and Eve through whom all people trace their life. By grace, Noah was not another stone buried in the flood; he was the single stone on which the post-flood world stood.

Noah's new life and significance is noted for its length. For decades, he constructed the 450-foot-long ark in full view of his mocking neighbors. We, however, get to hear nothing from Noah during those years of faithful building. But we do get to hear from three very different men in Luke 18–19 who also had grace upend their worlds. Their stories give us the full effect of that transformation in word and actions. By comparing these three men, we can see that two of them were transformed when grace upended their worlds. One, however, remained completely in his deadly rut.

We begin this three-way comparison with the rich ruler (Luke 18:18–30). The ruler asked Jesus what he had to do to inherit eternal life (18:18). He didn't want to be overturned by grace. He wanted an ovation for the rut he was in. Jesus reminded him of the commandments, and the ruler insisted that he had done them all since his youth. Jesus then said that he needed only to sell his riches, give the proceeds to the poor, and follow Him. But the rich man couldn't be turned over by grace. His wealth of gold was a stone too heavy to be lifted and too bound to the earth to be overturned. He went away sorrowful for he never left the rut he had always been in. When he left Jesus, he was a gilded stone falling back into a deadly hole.

He was a gilded stone falling back into a deadly hole. But what a contrast of upending grace comes with the next two men. Completely opposite of the rich man in resources and ability was the blind beggar Bartimaeus, who called to Jesus for mercy (Luke 18:38–39). Jesus invited him to come forward, asked what he wanted, and then granted his request of renewed sight. "And immediately he recovered his sight and followed Him, glorifying God. And all the people, when they saw it, gave praise to God" (Luke 18:43). The beggar had no money. He had no mobility to pursue Jesus and certainly no social standing to command Jesus' attention. Bartimaeus lacked all those things that the ruler possessed, but he was the stone turned over by grace. Imagine how immediately his story changed. He went from woe to joy. His pockets were likely still empty. It didn't matter. After all, empty pockets are more easily turned upside down and inside out. This man showed how grace could not only overturn one's life but also how grace could cause a former stone to leap out of his rut.

To give the final contrast in this trio, we need Zacchaeus. Zacchaeus, the rich tax collector, is perhaps an expected bend in the contextual river. In Luke 18, we saw a rich ruler and then a poor blind beggar. The rich ruler rejected the offer of grace, but the beggar took it gladly. In Luke 19, Zacchaeus combined aspects of these two previous men in a distinctive way. Like both other men, he desired to see Jesus. However, unlike them, he never said a word and called no attention to himself. Seated in the tree to see Jesus pass, Zacchaeus likely wanted only to see and not be seen. But Jesus called him. The other two men began their time with Jesus by asking Him a question. But with Zacchaeus, Jesus simply commanded him to come down for He, Jesus, must stay at his house that night (Luke 19:5). Grace upended Zacchaeus's world! Immediately, he hurried down and welcomed Jesus. We can imagine that there was no expense spared and that his banquet was a real-life example of that which the father hosted for his returned prodigal son in Luke 15.

What Zacchaeus did next showed the full extent of his overturned life. I would guess that many people must have wondered how much money Zacchaeus had. His wealth was likely a gold and silver iceberg, 90 percent hidden from view. For his own safety, as a hated tax collector, Zacchaeus probably didn't speak of his wealth. But grace upended even a rich man's world. What the rich ruler couldn't do when commanded, Zacchaeus largely did by the prompting of grace. "Behold, Lord, the half of my goods I give to the poor. And if I have defrauded anyone of anything, I restore it fourfold" (Luke 19:8). When Zacchaeus was overturned by grace, his fortune went from being a bitter, hidden nugget to a shining treasure chest, broken open and handed out as grace changed his world.

CAN'T YOU STAY?

When you're visiting someone, and it seems time to leave, you get up and start heading for the door. To be polite, your hosts say, "Can't you stay?" What do you say? This takes wisdom. Maybe they're only saying it because that's what you are supposed to say. In that case, they're hoping you go. Other times, they really mean it. "Can't you stay?" In fact, that's often exactly what you've been hoping to hear. But you can't first say, "Say, you know, I could stay awhile. Do you want me to?" No, it has to start with your host saying, "Can't you stay?"

We just saw Zacchaeus host Jesus for that evening meal and perhaps for the night that followed. When Jesus left, we can imagine that Zacchaeus said, in essence, "Can't You stay?" With no record of a lengthy stay, we can only assume that Jesus moved on after that one evening. But for a lengthy stay that epitomized grace upending the world, we have our final example of two women contrasted by a man. As with Luke 18 and 19, we will first have a long moment of doubt and distance followed by two who embrace the change that comes with grace. With these three, we have instant evidence of the power of grace and God's call to change one's world.

It all began with Zechariah in Luke 1 when the angel Gabriel announced that finally he and his wife, Elizabeth, would have a child. This incredible gift of grace would upend their world, so we might expect that Zechariah welcomed the news. But instead he asked, with what must have been a doubting tone, how he would know this. His long decades of disappointment had conditioned him to doubt. And so the verdict came. The baby, John the Baptist, would come, but Zechariah would be mute for the nine months of Elizabeth's pregnancy. Their lives would be upended, but a remnant of their past would remain. We might suspect that Zechariah and Elizabeth no longer spoke of having children in their last years. What a sad silence they endured those many years. But during the nine months of waiting for John's birth, the silence was broken only in part. Elizabeth was joyfully turned by grace from silence to thanks. Zechariah was still held down by the rut of silence, but that would eventually end.

The silence is broken when Elizabeth and Mary meet in Luke 1. The angel Gabriel told Mary the astonishing news of the Messiah coming to her by the conception by the Holy Spirit. Her faithful acceptance led her to travel to Elizabeth, the one person who could especially understand her amazing news. As she entered the house, John the Baptist leaped in Elizabeth's womb. What a great moment of life upturned by the gift of grace! Elizabeth exclaimed her wonder that the mother of her Lord would come to her. Then Mary sang the words of the Magnificat. With the inspired leaping of John, the faith-filled welcome and wonder by Elizabeth, and the timeless song of Mary, grace upends the world. This moment with all three involved shows perhaps best the readiness for the gift of grace. Also this trio of reactions displays much of that which was still hidden to the world but seen by faith in the text of Luke. By the gift of the Spirit's revelation, John, Elizabeth, and Mary give us a first look at the treasure to be lifted up and given to the world in the coming birth of Jesus. Mary's visit with Elizabeth lasted only three joyful months. But that was only the beginning of the lasting stay of Jesus with the world. For all time, He has come to dwell with us, to overturn our lives by His grace.

My Uncle's Rock Collection

My uncle collected rocks. Given that our family picked rocks by the ton each spring but then dumped them in a ditch, my uncle's love of rocks stood out. He would go over to the rock pile and find ones that interested him. He would tell us what kind they were and would then put them in his tumbler, that rotisserie for rocks that turns them over and over. Amazing results! He would come back and show us the stones that meant nothing to us but were beautiful when patiently turned.

The grace that upends our world is a bit like a rock tumbler. Mary did this in Luke 2:19 at the end of Christmas Eve night. After the shepherds had left, "Mary treasured up all these things, pondering them in her heart." The verb *pondering* is συμβάλλω (*symballō*), which is two Greek words, the prefix σύν (*syn*) meaning "together" or "with" and the verb βάλλω (*ballō*) meaning "to throw." So συμβάλλω (*symballō*) is to throw something together; to throw it back and forth, such as in a conversation; or if done by yourself, to juggle—to ponder. Mary took these amazing events of the last nine months and pondered them, turning them over and over, polishing them to reveal the treasure that they were.

So this gift of grace that overturns our world needs patient polishing. The gift in itself is perfect. The nature of grace is that it is the downward gift of God that enters our home as we are. Zacchaeus didn't ask Jesus to wait for half an hour so he could first clean up. Jesus entered the house as it was. So the gift of grace that comes to us in Baptism and by hearing the Word is perfectly complete in itself.

However, the full beauty of the perfect gift of grace takes patience and faith. It takes enormous faith, given by grace itself, to be lifted upward out of our past rut. Faith alone allows us to let go of the entangling roots that have kept us where and how we are. We might not be called to the adventures of Moses, Ruth, or Mary, but for us the steps we take likely seem just as daring. So God likely moves us step by step. Each step is a tumbling, turn by turn, polishing our understanding of His grace. By patient steps and turns, God shows us His full intention. But in the end, grace comes to upend our world, to show the mercy of God, His uplifting power, and the beauty of His promises.

> Each step is a tumbling, turn by turn, polishing our understanding of His grace.

"BY GRACE I'M SAVED"

While hymns of grace are many, and we might easily have chosen "Amazing Grace," the hymn "By Grace I'm Saved" (*LSB* 566) by Christian Ludwig Scheidt captures the tension between the offer of grace and our reaction. Notice in stanza 1 how the coming of grace leads to natural questions:

By grace I'm saved, grace free and boundless;
> My soul, believe and doubt it not.
Why stagger at this word of promise?
> Has Scripture ever falsehood taught?
No! Then this word must true remain:
By grace you too will life obtain.

The power of God's grace to calm our questions and fears comes out in stanza 5. Here we find both a challenging turn of life and also a sure anchor.

By grace to timid hearts that tremble,
> In tribulation's furnace tried,
By grace, in spite of fear and trouble,
> The Father's heart is open wide.
Where could I help and strength secure
If grace were not my anchor sure?

In the end of life, grace will be that which lifts us from this earth to the promise that never ends. The final stanza expresses this certainty also:

By grace! On this I'll rest when dying;
> In Jesus' promise I rejoice;
For though I know my heart's condition,
> I also know my Savior's voice.
My heart is glad, all grief has flown
Since I am saved by grace alone.

Discussion Questions

1. Several times this chapter spoke of the boring job of picking rocks on the farm. What was a similar job for you, either as a child or adult? Despite being a boring job, what good still came from doing that job?

2. In a similar way, how might grace be seen as God drawing us into a difficult, challenging life, making bricks without straw, so to speak?

3. What are some of the most common objections we might have to the changes in our life that God's grace would bring?

4. Another image of this chapter was the pet that joyfully became part of your family. When did you have a pet that was right at home, perhaps faster than you ever imagined?

5. So also how does God's grace surprisingly welcome us into His presence?

6. This chapter used several biblical examples of those who resisted the offer of God's grace. Besides the people discussed here, who else comes to mind as one who put off the offers of God? On the other hand, who joyfully followed the gracious calling of God?

7. In what ways does God's grace demand patience on our part? Why doesn't God simply give us instant perfection when His surprising grace comes to us?

CHAPTER 6

WHAT DOES GREATNESS LOOK LIKE?

No one was impressed when they met him, for there was nothing remarkable about Ulysses S. Grant. Despite being the general who largely won the Civil War for the Union, Grant left people wondering when they first met him. The historian Bruce Catton described Grant this way:

> The Governor of Illinois remembered that "he was plain, very plain," and men said that he usually went about camp in a short blue coat and an old slouch hat, wearing nothing that indicated his rank, nothing indeed that even proved he was in the Army. . . . There was nothing about Ulysses S. Grant that struck the eye; and this puzzled people, after it was all over, because it seemed reasonable that greatness, somewhere along the line, should look like greatness. Grant could never look like anything, and he could never make the things he did look very special; and afterward men could remember nothing more than the fact that when he came around things seemed to happen. (Bruce Catton, *Grant Moves South* [Boston: Little, Brown and Company, 1960], 3.)

How should greatness appear? Can we recognize it in some reliable way? With Grant, that would have been difficult. We might have not even known he was a soldier and certainly wouldn't have guessed he was a four-star general. Furthermore, Grant made little effort to be known as great, at least in his clothes and manners. Yet that good judge of character Abraham Lincoln saw in him what others missed and promoted him above all his contemporaries. Greatness can be seen, if you know what to look for.

How can we recognize biblical greatness? There are certainly moments that shout glory and greatness. Shouldn't God come with a power that everyone can see? Shouldn't His perfection be so obvious that no one can doubt it? Shouldn't His answers come with a wisdom that dazzles even the brightest mind? I think we would all agree to that and be glad to see it. Let God show a perfect, instant greatness.

In making that request, we likely are making a promise about ourselves. If God would only show His glory in an unmistakable way, then we promise to see Him, praise Him, and follow Him. This is the promise that has been made repeatedly in the Scriptures, and we will trace many of those promises. At times, we've even kept part of our promises, at least for a time. It all makes sense: let God be God in all His glory and we'll be obedient followers.

But there is another side of God's greatness that doesn't match this plan. That's the hidden greatness that God uses far more than we might expect. God can speak with thunder and lightning, earthquake and fire, but often He prefers to whisper. God can send lightning and fire from heaven for everyone to see, but often He prefers to send one frightened man to speak for Him instead. God can dazzle the crowd with angels in heaven, singing a mighty chorus. But He ultimately prefers to be found in a stable, lying in a manger, with no chorus to be heard except the sound of the animals that share the stable with Him.

Perhaps we might see these two sides in the description of Grant. The setting, the actions, and the reaction to what God does might not match our expectations for a miraculous God. However, we might find that the work is still done. As with Grant, the outward appearance was not impressive, yet battles were won when he was around. Grant didn't particularly care if you knew his rank. He wasn't there for his own fame but for the fighting that had to be done. So also we find the same principle with the work of God through many of His people. God showed His power in the work that was done, even if no flashy drama surrounded that work.

In fact, God's hidden work best expresses the nature of God's relationship with us. If we demand glory, what happens to faith? Faith lives with invisible hope. But the greatness that leaps up when heavenly fire comes down, that greatness must put on an ever-increasing display. Each day's demonstration of God's glory must eclipse the next. If a dark day comes, we could dismiss God. He failed to meet our demands.

But the true nature of God comes through hidden greatness, and with that comes His relationship built on patient faith. Faith both sees what is there and trusts what is to come. Faith recognizes the greatness in shadow and silence. Faith hears the whisper of God more clearly than the whiplash of His thunder. Faith sees God's full power in a tiny baby without deducting for the length of His manger.

Faith also trusts what is still to come. When Grant was in the field, he generally wore the simplest uniform, even the private's coat as Bruce Catton described. Pictures of him in the field often show him with no general's insignia or sword. But there are later pictures of Grant in full uniform such as when he was presented formally to President Lincoln in the White House. Then he wore all the regalia that he was due.

So faith trusts that glory might come in a way that can be seen. God will have His day of return in which every knee will bow and every tongue confess that Jesus is Lord to the glory of God the Father (Philippians 2:10–11). Then the patience of faith can rise up and say, "I knew it. I saw it coming. I was certain He would do everything He said."

This confidence is a natural flow from our previous theme, "Grace Upends Our World." In that theme, we lived by faith in the promise of grace. Yes, our world was upside down, but this was out of grace, not condemnation. That grace promises us that our lives will be transformed by God's mercy and His power will move us closer to Himself. Trusting this promise, we look for evidence that life is being renewed by grace. Life should become better, not bitter.

The balance to this view comes with our question in this theme, "What Does Greatness Look Like?" We know many biblical examples of outward greatness, so we expect outward greatness to be reflected in ourselves. Perhaps we'll join the line of biblical people who've been dramatically healed, remarkably rescued, and instantly transformed. However, this theme reminds us that God has shown another greatness through His still, small voice, His enduring relationship with His people, and His filling of the darkness of the cross and tomb.

At this point, many readers will be saying, "Isn't this theme an exercise in the theology of glory versus theology of the cross?" There are aspects of the theology of glory and theology of the cross that help us see this theme at work. Theology of glory looks for a visible demonstration of God's power, a display of power that brings outward peace, success, and fame. Theology of glory expresses the outward wisdom of the world in 1 Corinthians 1:22–24: "For Jews demand signs and Greeks seek wisdom, but we preach Christ crucified, a stumbling block to Jews and folly to Gentiles, but to those

> Faith hears the whisper of God more clearly than the whiplash of His thunder.

who are called, both Jews and Greeks, Christ the power of God and the wisdom of God." A theology of glory expects God to bring a relatively immediate perfection, which is the opposite of suffering. Luther describes this contrast: "He who does not know Christ does not know God hidden in suffering. Therefore he prefers works to suffering, glory to the cross, strength to weakness, wisdom to folly, and, in general, good to evil" (AE 31:53). Theology of glory always expects glory to be demonstrated outwardly and quickly. It is the first cousin to our early theme of instant perfection without any place given for having a patient relationship. Theology of glory seeks the tangible gift from God as most important, not the relationship with God. Theology of glory wants a demonstration sent by God, not a patient walk beside God. God's miracle, however, is that He shows His greatness in the small steps that He takes with us.

Consider the difference between winning a race and walking a child. Here at Concordia University Wisconsin, I've had the chance to watch many outstanding athletes compete, including all-Americans in track and field and cross-country. I've watched them race first across the finish line, beating hundreds of others. They are truly impressive—and if you want a dose of humility, run beside one of these all-Americans on a treadmill. Run your best pace and then sneak a peek over to the pace display on their treadmill. How can she run so fast, no effort, talking with you like she was sitting down? Well, she is an all-American.

But that was a few years ago. Now watch that same all-American walk with her child as her one-year-old takes her first steps. She's posted the video on YouTube. How fast is her pace now? How big is the crowd that's watching? How loud are the cheers? There's none of that. She's a mom walking with her one-year-old. And if you ask, she'll tell you that those few slow steps holding her daughter's hand are more significant than many a race that she won. Where is greatness found? It is not only in the breathtaking speed of an all-American but even more in the patient walk of a one-year-old's mother.

So in this chapter, we will see both definitions of greatness as God works through His people and as He expresses His own nature both to them and through them. We'll be glad to see those moments when God unveils all that we might expect of His glory and even more. But we are especially looking forward to seeing the greatness that comes quietly in the dark and whispers our name. The uniform of His greatness is in the humble clothes they snatched away and the grave clothes in which He lay.

I Know What I'm Looking For

When I go to a big home improvement store, I get lost. I thought I knew where the screws were and then the stain, but they must have changed things around. I have that look that says, "It's got to be here somewhere, but could somebody help me?" Unfortunately, usually there's no one around to see that look. I know what screws are, and I can see in my mind that bright yellow can of stain. It's just not in my hand yet.

As frustrating as this experience can be, it's better than having something broken at home but you don't know what will fix it. You go to the store with just the dim hope that there must be something on some aisle that will fix your problem. You need something, but you don't know exactly what to call it. And you don't know if you'll recognize it when you see it. But you trust that it's in the store.

God's greatness is like both of these examples. We're going to start with the greatness that we have seen or at least have imagined. It's like wandering through the ultimate big-box store of God's creation, looking for a greatness we can recognize. We know the glory

> The uniform of His greatness is in the humble clothes they snatched away and the grave clothes in which He lay.

we're expecting to find, and often we won't be disappointed. God will give us the greatness that can be seen. In those moments, we might see a reflected image of Himself with the majesty that we expect.

The Light Bulbs Are by the Door

The big box stores I know begin a bit like the greatness of God in Genesis 1. Light bulbs are the first things you see by the door. There must be a marketing strategy that says people don't come to the store for light bulbs, but if they see them they won't leave without them. So the greatness we expect with God is light, His first act of creation in Genesis 1:3. God's bright greatness continues with the distinct lights of the stars, sun, and moon, and the division of night and day in Genesis 1:14–19, the fourth day. Our association with God comes also with the sixth-day creation of Adam and Eve as a reflection of God's light shining upon us.

Those initial moments of God's light shape our expectation of divine greatness. But the light of God that began in Eden has more than one shape and reflection. Job 38, for example, shows God essentially retracing the days of creation as He challenges Job to know and command the elements of the earth. In Job 38:12–15, God asks who commanded the morning and made the dawn know its place. Later in verses 31–33, God demands if Job knows his way through the heavenly stars and constellations and commands them into their places. These challenges remind us that the lights of creation are still the mark of God's glory. "Praise Him, sun and moon, praise Him, all you shining stars" (Psalm 148:3).

The light that comes from God, which defines glory, can be intense. When I was a boy on the farm, my father welded metal while I held the pieces and watched. Dad loved to weld using a red Lincoln electric arc welder, the kind of machine that started with a jolt and seemed to dim all the lights in the shop. The intense blue flame of the welder was too much to watch, so Dad used a welding helmet with a dark visor. But as the helper who was only supposed to hold the metal pieces together, I didn't wear a helmet. Dad only said, "Don't look." But saying that was just a little boy's reason to look. That fierce blue welding light was fascinating. It was fire melting metal. So I watched and later wondered when the bright blue spots I was seeing would go away.

Moses finds that kind of intense, lingering light. The burning bush was a light that defines the glory of God. "And the angel of the LORD appeared to him in a flame of fire out of the midst of a bush. He looked, and behold, the bush was burning, yet it was not consumed" (Exodus 3:2). Here is an intersection between God and His creation, a fiery union that draws Moses in so God could speak the commissioning words that would send Moses back to Egypt. This brilliant fire defines the kind of glory from God that we expect.

The light that defines God can also be seen easily in the contest of Elijah and the prophets of Baal in 1 Kings 18. Here God defines Himself and His greatness by bringing fire from heaven. Elijah gathers the people of Israel and demands that they decide whom they will follow, God or Baal. Elijah makes this comparison a clear challenge: "'And you call upon the name of your god, and I will call upon the name of the LORD, and the God who answers by fire, He is God.' And all the people answered, 'It is well spoken'" (1 Kings 18:24). As we know, Elijah waits for the utter failure of Baal to send fire, and then he prays simply, briefly, and God sends fire to devour the sacrifice, wood, stone, and water. The God who defines Himself by creative light defends Himself with consuming fire.

This light with Elijah is the brief, intense light that distinguishes friend from foe, much like that motion-sensitive, intense light that guards your front entrance. That intensity is increased even more with the next expectations of God's glory in light. Jesus identifies Himself as the light of the world (John 8:12). When He first arrives, we expect light that demonstrates His glory. We're not disappointed as the glory of God shatters the calm darkness of the shepherds' watch on Christmas Eve (Luke 2:9). This great light likely increased as the whole chorus of heaven joined in song (Luke 2:13). Here, greatness is defined by every light in heaven.

> The God who defines Himself by creative light defends Himself with consuming fire.

But the great lights of Christmas can't always be on. Most of our Christmas lights get put away, even though your neighbor keeps his icicle lights dangling from the roof all year long. Our

Christmas lights are usually hidden in the dark corner of the basement closet until we go looking for them the day after Thanksgiving. So the glory that we see through the angelic Christmas lights is put away throughout much of Jesus' ministry. His humility was a darkening shade over the light He could have shown. The disciples were likely so accustomed to this humility that they were unprepared for the display that would come in the transfiguration. There Jesus unveiled most clearly His defining light. Mark described Him this way: "And He was transfigured before them, and His clothes became radiant, intensely white, as no one on earth could bleach them" (Mark 9:2–3). He shone with a light that truly set Him apart from others. The Pharisees might have aspired to be those set apart by their acts of holiness. But no Pharisee fantasy could match His transfigured light.

Here is the culmination of the light that we cannot bear but which defines God. Here is the light that shone around Moses on Mount Sinai so that the fire of the mountain warned of God's presence: "The glory of the LORD dwelt on Mount Sinai. . . . Now the appearance of the glory of the LORD was like a devouring fire on the top of the mountain" (Exodus 24:16–17). Moses' face reflected that glory when he returned from the second forty-day stay upon the mountain so that "the skin of his face shone because he had been talking with God" (Exodus 34:29). The expected displays of glory leave us expecting a greater display when Jesus Himself is in ministry. It's fitting that in the transfiguration, we have the true light that defines visible glory. And yet, it is a light that needs no protecting shade. It is interesting that there is no caution spoken to the disciples in the transfiguration accounts. They weren't warned to turn their eyes away but could endure this dazzling light. You can't bear to watch electric arc welding, but they could see the glory of God shine

No Pharisee fantasy could match His transfigured light.

through His flesh. John summed up this bearable intersection: "The Word became flesh and dwelt among us, and we have seen

His glory, glory as of the only Son from the Father, full of grace and truth" (John 1:14).

The lingering light of the transfiguration should have shone well into the journey that followed. In our liturgical year, Transfiguration Sunday is the Sunday before Lent begins. What a perfect time to let the brightness of transfiguration go with us. Let the greatness seen in that mountain be the constant light for the disciples and us as we walk into the darkening days leading to the cross.

I WISH I KNEW THE STORY

When you're driving down the road, you see the runner on the road's shoulder. There's a story there. No matter how tired he looks or how fast he's going, there's a story about him. There's a "before" image to this moment, and I wish I could see it. He's flying along now with a fluid style and a lightning pace. But was he always that way? Was he once the slowest kid in his class, the one who hated running? Or was he the one who blew out his knee, had the surgery a year ago, and has fought through the rehab pain to be running like this today? I wish I knew the story because this moment of beautiful running may be built on the daring of a last-place child who chose to keep running when everyone else had gone in. I wish I could see them both run side by side, that struggling child and the man he would come to be. Both of them would be a picture of greatness.

Biblical greatness is both of these runners. We expect God to run His course with speed and grace and leave us in awe. We expect Him to scale the mountains and walk on the sea. We join the crowd to cheer as He comes to the finish line of Palm Sunday praise. But we also want to see the earlier images, the ones on which His final steps are built. He is the infant carried in Mary's womb on the journey from Nazareth to Bethlehem. He is the infant carried in Mary's arms into the temple and then in haste to Egypt for His safekeeping. He is the twelve-year-old walking confidently through Jerusalem's streets directly to the temple. Perhaps when I next see a runner along the road, I can see both images of greatness, the child and the man, the slow and the flying, the victorious and the left-behind. And in those two images, I see God's two dimensions of greatness.

By Now, It's Turned Pink

I just retired my old motorcycle jacket and pants, a pair that I have worn for just over five years. I have 100,000 miles of riding in them now, and they look it. The jacket was red when new. But it's faded to pink now, and in with the pink there is a ground-in layer of grit that won't wash out. This coat is not pretty. But it's perfect.

In the motorcycle world, there's a school of thought that believes stained pink is the perfect color for a coat. It takes a lot of sunshine, rain, and riding over tens of thousands of miles to turn red into that shade of pink. Nobody has to ask if you ride very much. Just look at the coat. A dirty pink coat gets respect. (By the way, my new jacket looks really sharp. It's clean and bright, and I look like a complete newbie wearing it.)

Maybe you've had the same experience with your clothes. Play football in the mud or run a race in a downpour, and your clothes will prove that you've done something. Afterward, you hold up the jersey and say, "Look at this. It was terrible out there." And you're proud of it.

Sometimes greatness wears mud-stained clothes. U. S. Grant wore a private's coat, mud-splattered with no general's stars on it. That was his greatness. So also the greatness that we can see in the Scriptures might come with many shades short of stunning white. The shades of greatness take a particular set of eyes to see, and perhaps we can only see that sort of greatness with a great deal of patience. In just the right, dim light, God displays a greatness that those with faith can see.

Colors Guaranteed to Fade

Red fades to pink. Aerostich, the company I buy my motorcycle jacket and pants from, warns you that red will turn to pink. It might be nice if they could say: "These colors will not fade." But we know they will.

Oddly enough, one of the first signs of God's greatness and displays of His character has colors guaranteed to fade. The rainbow is a sign of God's mercy and His promise that He will never again strike the earth. "I have set my bow in the cloud, and it shall be a sign of the covenant between Me and the earth" (Genesis 9:13). Certainly a sign set in the heavens, visible to all, might define greatness for many. But this is a strange sign since it is set in the clouds themselves, the clouds being the source of the destruction of the flood. We might imagine His sign to be a mountain towering into the clouds, fixed as a place of refuge. But God shows His glory in the cloud. He turns what might have been the darkness of judgment into the pastels of promise. These colors are only for a moment—how often have you seen a rainbow, run inside, gotten everyone outside to see it, but by then it's almost completely gone? "Well, it looked a lot better before" is all you can say. So God is content with His promise being briefly seen in fading colors.

Of course, you have to know what you're seeing to appreciate the rainbow's message. That message is God's gracious gift to Noah and the world. However, God also shows His hidden greatness when asked in confrontation. When greatness is expected on the largest scale, God can instead answer in a hidden way that unnerves the one who dares to ask Him for a sign.

Elijah might be the best example of this transformation from bold request to stunned fear. We remembered earlier the dramatic show of perfect power in 1 Kings 18 when Elijah called down fire from heaven. There was greatness looking like greatness! But the following chapter shows the hidden greatness of God's endurance and kindness. Immediately after the miracle of fire from heaven, Queen Jezebel threatened Elijah with death. We might have thought she would be moved to repentance by the heavenly fire. But she was as coldhearted as ever. So Elijah retreated to the desert, complaining to God, "It is enough; now, O LORD, take away my life" (1 Kings 19:4). Instead of answering Elijah's complaint with power, God answered Elijah with cake and water, letting him rest before setting out on a forty-day journey into the desert. Instead of the instant perfection of fiery judgment on Jezebel, God baked a cake over hot stones and walked patiently into the desert with Elijah. When this was over, Elijah reached the cave at Mount Horeb, and God spoke with him. Elijah renewed his complaint that he alone was left. God told him to stand at the mouth of cave. Next came the progressive display of what might be the glory of God. A wind tore the mountains and broke apart rocks, but God was not in it. An earthquake shook the ground, but God was not in that. A fire raged, but God was not in the fire. Then came the sound of a low whisper that brought the words of God, words that sent Elijah back to work with the promise that seven thousand people still held to the faith. One faithful God had journeyed with him for forty days, sending him back to seven thousand people who still waited for his return.

> He turns what might have been the darkness of judgment into the pastels of promise.

The Key Is Hidden in the Coat

My motorcycle jackets have eight outside pockets. I use three of them every day—keys in one, wallet and phone in another, garage door opener in the third. The others are just there, holding nothing but dust and a ticket to the races at Road America two years ago. But then there's the smallest pocket high on the left side. That's where I keep the spare keys for each bike. I forget all about that tiny pocket and the keys until I need one of them, like the time when I was two hundred miles from home and couldn't find my bike key when it was time to go. Thank goodness the spare key was hiding in that tiny pocket. At that moment, the most important place in my world was the tiny, dark opening that hid the key.

The still, small voice in the dark cave was that strange greatness, the hidden key. For Elijah, nothing had changed, but everything was different. He went back, though Jezebel was as murderous as ever. But Elijah had heard God's mercy and found God's greatness in a hidden pocket. Thanks to that tiny cave, Elijah found the key to take his journey back.

Another case of hidden greatness involves another cave, or something much like it. If we have the still, small voice of God coming to Elijah in a cave, we might expect the contextual river to bring us to another such meeting. Christmas is that moment. Many commentators suggest that the stable in which Jesus was born was either a cave or a cave-like structure that was the lower level of a house. How fitting that God used this setting to display His incarnate Son for the first time. In Luke 2:10–12, the angel told the frightened shepherds where to see His glory: "And this will be a sign for you: you will find a baby wrapped in swaddling cloths and lying in a manger" (v. 12). This is not the sign of greatness we expect. The following verses tell of the sky opening, the whole chorus of angels appearing, and the Gloria in Excelsis being sung. That's greatness. But that was not the confirming sign of the Christmas message. The sign that assured the shepherds was this: a baby lying in a manger. No blazing light shone there, only perhaps the light of an oil lamp. But in that stillness, God was seen and heard in the small voice of a just-born baby. There was greatness for those with eyes to see it.

The Pink Coat Is Still in the Basement

I haven't thrown away my pink coat. First of all, how could I? It's been my friend for these last five years. The adventures we've had! Also, I might need it. What if our son Steve comes home and we go riding together? He can wear my new coat, and I'll wear the old one. I know I probably should get rid of it, but for now it's hanging in the basement, and I'm keeping it.

That's what God also did to display His greatness. What should have been gone got to stay. God's greatness is not always in the creation of something new but in the preserving of something old. We see this first in the rebellion of Numbers 14. The people of Israel in their exodus journey have despaired of ever entering the Promised Land and have demanded new leaders instead of Moses. God says to Moses, "I will strike them with the pestilence and disinherit them, and I will make of you a nation greater and mightier than they" (Numbers 14:12). That would be a sign of glory to rival the plagues in Egypt and the crossing of the Red Sea.

But Moses cannot bear to see them cast away and destroyed. He argues with God that He can't do this. The Egyptians will hear of it and conclude that God is unable to bring Israel into the land. Instead of being a sign of power, this destruction would be a proof of weakness. So God relents and allows that generation to live, though they'll never enter the Promised Land. Moses sums up the true power of God this way: "And now, please let the power of the Lord be great as You have promised, saying, 'The LORD is slow to anger and abounding in steadfast love, forgiving iniquity and transgression'" (Numbers 14:17–18). The power of God is not only in the moments of new creation but also in the moments of patient forbearance. Here is the quiet greatness of steadfast love. God lets these people remain, continues to feed them, guide them, and bring from them the generation that will enter the Promised Land.

When we have seen God do this with Moses, we might well expect that we will see this again in Jesus' ministry. Perhaps the clearest parallel is in the encounter of Jesus with the people of Nazareth (Luke 4:16–30). Jesus came to Nazareth after performing miracles for the people of Capernaum, a much larger, generally Gentile city. He returned to His native home and proclaimed in the synagogue that the prophecy of Isaiah 61:1–2 had been fulfilled by Him that day. The town of Nazareth grumbled that He did miracles for the Gentiles of Capernaum and not for them. So they took Jesus to the brow of the hill outside town to throw Him down to His death. But He walked through the midst of them and went away.

It seems there is no miracle here, no greatness or glory to be seen. But consider the greatness when God does nothing. There is glory in walking away. Remember what happened earlier in this chapter. During Jesus' temptation, the devil took Him to the pinnacle of the temple and urged Him to step off so the angels might carry Him safely down. That would be glory for everyone in the temple court to see. But Jesus said, "You shall not put the Lord your God to the test" (Luke 4:12). Then a few verses later, Jesus was on another cliff outside Nazareth. Perhaps there Jesus would demonstrate His power in an unmistakable way. Imagine what He could have done: Turn everyone who touched Him to stone; step off the cliff and hover in midair before them; glare at them with the blazing eyes of a wrathful God. That would show the greatness that we'd expect.

But the true greatness was the simplicity of Jesus' walking through the crowd, leaving them whole. The mercy with which He spared His town was a foretaste of the greater mercy to come. On that day outside His hometown of Nazareth, He showed greatness by doing nothing, harming no one, and walking away. On another day, a greater mercy and glory would be seen. On a darker day outside His ultimate city Jerusalem, another crowd rushed Him to a hill to kill Him. He did not pass through their midst unharmed that time. He did not display His glory as they jeeringly demanded. He did not harm them, but neither did He protect Himself. His greatness was shown by the quiet

> **Consider the greatness when God does nothing.**

acceptance of His death. His greatness was shown in the darkness that surrounded His final hours. His greatness wore no uniform for His clothes had been gambled away. His greatness had no light by which He could be seen. His greatness could only be seen with eyes of faith.

DID GRANT KEEP THE COAT?

I wonder if General Grant kept the private's coat he wore in camp during the war. After the war, Grant was a two-term president and no longer wore his general's uniform. I would like to think that Julia, his wife, kept the old coat somewhere and that it was brought out with warm memories for the days spent in camp. Let Grant wear a suit fit for a president, but the old coat should still be in the closet.

Just as Grant likely had both his general's uniform and his presidential suit, the greatness of Jesus has an even more wonderful both/and in this regard. So far, we have been using the two sides of this theme as generally distinct. Either God has shown His glory in a way that we expect and can see, or He has hidden His greatness in a manner only faith can see. But in the Easter appearances, Jesus brings these two dimensions together. When He appears to the disciples after passing through the walls of their room, the disciples are in awe. Then Jesus shows them the wounds in His hands and His side. What a combination of glory and the cross! Greatness as we expect has risen from the dead and comes instantly through the barriers of doors and walls. But perhaps greater greatness is in His wounds. These marks are not cast away as signs of weakness but are the genuine glory of His sacrifice and love. These marks identify Him to a doubting Thomas. These wounds bring healing for us. A president cannot wear a muddy private's coat to a state dinner. But the risen Savior, glorious in His perfect, lasting resurrection, carries still the nail-wrought wounds. In that, greatness looks like greatness.

Our hope is to have eyes to see that greatness in all its ways. We might want a greatness that dazzles us instantly, but we likely couldn't bear to watch it. But God comes with a gentle light, a caring greatness that tells His story with a whisper. Lord, let us hear Your still voice and give us patience to see Your glory in darkness and light.

"FROM HEAVEN ABOVE TO EARTH I COME"

The wonderful contrast of radiant glory and hidden majesty comes through many hymns, especially Christmas carols. Martin Luther's hymn "From Heaven Above to Earth I Come" (*LSB* 358) beautifully describes the opposites of Christ's Christmas greatness. Luther describes Jesus' coming as a wonderful exchange in stanza 8. The baby who is born knows that He will not only share our most humble home but will take our most painful sins:

> Welcome to earth, O noble Guest,
>
> Through whom the sinful world is blest!
>
> You came to share my misery
>
> That You might share Your joy with me.

In stanzas 10 and 11, Luther contrasts the humble setting of the stable with what should be given to a king. No matter what we might have done to prepare for Him, it would not have been enough. But He came completely apart from any work we could have done:

> Were earth a thousand times as fair
>
> And set with gold and jewels rare,
>
> It would be far too poor and small
>
> A cradle for the Lord of all.

> Instead of soft and silken stuff
>
> You have but hay and straw so rough
>
> On which as King, so rich and great,
>
> To be enthroned in royal state.

We will always stand in wonder as the King chooses to come to the lowest place and call that His preferred home. In stanza 13, one final contrast comes when Luther expresses the hope we all have. Let Jesus come, not only to the stable and manger, but also to each of us:

Ah, dearest Jesus, holy Child,

Prepare a bed, soft, undefiled,

A quiet chamber set apart

For You to dwell within my heart.

DISCUSSION QUESTIONS

1. The chapter began with the story of General Grant and his casual dress. He showed a strange greatness. Who else in your experience has shown a similar humble appearance in contrast to the impressive clothes he might have worn?

2. Light was used as the natural display of glory in the chapter. What is it about light that makes it a natural expression of divine glory?

3. What biblical episodes showed the glory of God through light? This could be historical events or more timeless expressions such as Psalm 27:1.

4. How does greatness that looks like greatness, as we expect, match in many ways the first half of our theme of instant perfection?

5. In the second half of the chapter, the faded pink coat was used. What clothes have you worn until they're faded like that? Have you thrown that piece out, or is it still in the closet?

6. How is the hidden glory of Jesus, especially the glory in His cross and scars, a glory created through long, hard miles and unseen service?

7. When the glory of God's work is hidden, camouflaged by hardship and service, why does it take patience to see and appreciate this as true greatness?

CHAPTER 7

GOD CURES WITH THE ILLNESS ITSELF

Picture a little green pot about three inches high and three inches wide. It's made of clay rolled into a rope and then circled upward, layer by layer. The clay was never smoothed out, so you can almost see the potter's fingerprints. It's too small and rough to be a cup; besides, there's no handle. It could have been an ash tray, but no one in the house smokes. It's just a sturdy, little green pot.

It sits on the shelf in our family room where it's been for some twenty years. That little green pot was our youngest daughter Nicole's Mother's Day gift for Holly back when Nicole was in third grade. It will never win a prize, but it will never lose its place. It doesn't have to do or be anything except a gift.

You made those gifts too. You were in kindergarten when the teacher gave you four colors of yarn and told you how to make Mom a corsage. There were probably wonderful, clear directions that involved various loops and twists. You missed the directions somehow, and so, trying to catch up with the other kids, you simply tied knots with the yarn, sometimes with two strings, sometimes with three strings. There were knots with knots inside the knots. And when you ran out of string, you were done. There, a corsage for Mom. But what did Mom say when you brought it home?

You walked in the house and said, "Here, Mom, happy Mother's Day." Your mother looked at the knot corsage and asked, "Did you make this?" You assured her you did, without any help from the teacher. She asked if you tied all those knots yourself, and you promised her that you did. And she said, "I'm putting it on right now." Of course that's safe. It's late Friday afternoon at home. But then Mom said, "And I'm going to wear it to church on Sunday."

And she did. Your mother wore your knot corsage on Sunday, at church and even at the restaurant afterward. Other mothers came up and asked, "Oh, did Amy make that for you?" And your mother said, "Yes, she did. Isn't it beautiful?" Of course, the other mothers said it was. And you got to hear it all.

I know this is an ideal story, and perhaps it didn't work out quite that way for you. Mom forgot the corsage, or she wore it under her sweater, pretty well hidden. And no mother needs to wear the knot corsage two Sundays in a row, so I hope you didn't ask her to wear it again. But let's say this: At our house, the little green rope pot is still on the shelf, and your mother really did wear the knot corsage that Mother's Day.

> It will never win a prize, but it will never lose its place.

Why? As we remember our gifts to our parents, there is no beauty or talent to be seen. No one suggested that you become an art major in college. And as we remember those projects now, we know not to ask our mothers, decades later, what happened to all the other things we made. It's enough that Mom wore that corsage that one Sunday. That corsage was more knots than yarn, but it was what Mom did with it and how she chose to see it that made it beautiful.

That is a large part of our chapter, "God Cures with the Illness Itself." We are more knot than yarn, more tangled mess than braided beauty. But what God does with us is the real story. We echo the words of 1 Peter 2:10: "Once you were not a people, but now you are God's people; once you had not received mercy, but now you have received mercy." God transformed the "nots" of our relationship so that we might be His people.

But how God does this is the wonder. Go back to the knotted corsage. Your little five-year-old fingers layered on knot after knot. If you wanted to undo those knots, it seemed you had two choices. First, you could try pulling on them. After all, it's only yarn with the knots of a five-year-old. Brute force should do it. Good luck. All the tugging in the world will only make that knot tighter. So also God could have demanded, threatened, and displayed all His power to straighten us out. He could have reminded us that we never followed His directions and that we are "knot" His people.

But He didn't do that. He also didn't do the other method—endless picking. A mass of knots will leave one loose string. Get something thin and sharp and just start picking at that one string. Picking at that one might open up another. Pick away long enough and maybe the knots will straighten out.

What endless picking God could have done on us! He might have had a relationship with us of constant picking, endless complaining, and a conversation that said nothing more than "Look what you've done now." But instead, He declares that we who deserved no mercy have now received mercy. We who were not His people, now we are His people.

It all comes down to that Mother's Day moment when Mom walked in wearing the knot corsage and someone asked, "Did Amy make that?" Mom didn't sigh or roll her eyes. She didn't have that look that said, "What are you going to do? It's Mother's Day." She immediately said, "Yes, yes, she did. Isn't it beautiful?" Yes, it is to a mother's eyes.

In the same way, we are lovely only to our heavenly Father. We are nothing but a nest of knots, not His people and not deserving His mercy. But He takes our knots and calls us His own. He wears us as His people. He allows His Son to fall into the twisted plans we have for Him. He allows His Son to be the ultimate example of the twisted, knotted serpent that heals us when we see Him. It is not His perfect beauty but His willingness to be lifted up in death that brings the healing of souls and the answer to death.

In this chapter, we'll explore the ways in which God heals with the illness itself. There's a wonderful biblical range in how God does this. At times, He works with those who have no idea that they are being used to accomplish His plans. Other times, it will seem that God is increasing the very problem itself, but it will be the increase that becomes the measure of the cure. Perhaps more often we will find that God confronts the evil itself and makes it an unwilling cure. Finally, God transforms the problem, especially the problem person, and in that transformation, the one who was the enemy becomes the ally.

This theme of curing by the illness itself is a wonderful turn in our tension between instant perfection and patient relationship. We are used to asking God to do His work and bring His answer, and we're conditioned by now to expect Him to say, "Be patient. The answer will come." But with this theme, the answer is already here. We'll hear the cry of God's people asking for relief while God's solution is already there in the problem itself. Since the answer came with the problem, we need to watch even more than wait. We may not see God's perfect use of the problem instantly. But we've been trained in His patience, and we know that the answer is at hand.

> But He takes our knots and calls us His own. He wears us as His people.

This One You Saved?

As I look at the little green pot, I wonder what happened to all the other projects the kids made. Certainly this wasn't the only ceramics class project. My file of kids' drawings has only a few sheets from each of the three kids. But in the early years, they must have brought home drawings every day. There was the flood of 1997 that ruined several boxes of school memories, but still, how did this pot and those few drawings last?

While I don't know the reason for these surviving, it raises the question that we might ask of God. Why did you save these moments and make them special? We'll see several actions that are clearly a problem. Some are an inconvenience at least, and others are pure evil at worst. Why are some preserved to become a solution while others simply pass on and are forgotten? Perhaps God has a significance and answer for every problem, and we'll see that in due time. Or perhaps only some are needed to be transformed into a solution, as we'll see. It depends on a patient relationship that trusts God's ongoing work to transform a problem into the solution.

The first example of this principle is when God uses someone's actions without them knowing it to turn an illness into a cure. There is distance between the actor and the result, and there is often a passing of time. Two biblical examples of this theme involve the leadership of nations. Joseph is sold into slavery by his brothers and then rises to become the second-in-command in Egypt. By this, he saves Egypt and also his own family from starvation in the seven-year famine. When his brothers no longer have the protection of their father, Jacob, they come to Joseph asking for mercy. Joseph responds with the famous words that show a transformation of their long-distant action: "As for you, you meant evil against me, but God meant it for good, to bring it about that many people should be kept alive, as they are today" (Genesis 50:20). The one who was oppressed became, by that very evil and oppression, the one who saved the oppressors.

> Since the answer came with the problem, we need to watch even more than wait.

The second example of this principle works on a larger scale in the New Testament. Mary was nine months pregnant in Nazareth and planned, we expect, to remain there for the delivery. But Caesar Augustus decreed that a census be taken of the whole world, so each had to return to their home city (Luke 2:1). This must have been seen as the worst news at the worst time for Mary and Joseph. But Caesar cared nothing for their danger and pain.

Yet this very evil became the means by which Jesus was born in Bethlehem, David's city, in order to fulfill the prophecy of Micah 5:2. The emperor could move the world, yet he knew nothing of those he moved. He sent this couple to a distant city where no one welcomed them except the angel chorus that sang with more glory than Caesar could imagine. The distant king ordered a census so that all the world might be taxed. But through that, a greater King was born to pay the debts of the world.

JUST HOLD THE BOARD

In these acts, the one who was carrying on the evil knew nothing of the consequence of his actions. The miles and years distanced the person from the consequence. Yet their action, which they did out of ignorance, was clear in God's plans. In another pair of examples, the evil that was done was fully aware of its effect but then had to see that effect reversed. Here God's action is more dramatically visible given the immediate presence of the evil.

When I was a boy on the farm, Dad and I often had to move rough cut lumber. We had stacks of boards—oak, tamarack, and elm—that were air drying in an old shed. The boards were eight to twelve feet long, heavy and rough as they had just come from the sawmill. Ideally, you would wear gloves handling them, but sometimes you just had to grab on with bare hands. But rough cut lumber is full of slivers just waiting for a little boy to come close.

I learned two things from handling those boards. First, grab on and don't let go. The more you move your hand up and down the board to find a place with no slivers, the more slivers you'll get. Just take the board as it comes to you. Second, notice how Dad is carrying the other end of the board. Only when I was older did I notice that Dad would pick up his end of the board near the middle. I was holding on to the last few inches at my end of the board. Of course, holding from near the middle, Dad was carrying much more of the weight. When I was little, I couldn't see the whole length of the board, so I assumed I was carrying at least half. But now I know Dad was carrying everything that I couldn't see.

I still got slivers in my hands, but these two rules helped. Stay with the sliver you have. And while I'm thinking I'm carrying some heroic load, Dad is carrying a whole lot more. Paul's thorn in the flesh is that oak board with all its slivers, not avoided but grasped. In 2 Corinthians 12:7, Paul describes the sharpness of this spiritual pin. "So to keep me from becoming conceited because of the surpassing greatness of the revelations, a thorn was given me in the flesh, a messenger of Satan to harass me, to keep me from becoming conceited." This sharp thorn was Satan's own tool, yet God turned it for a greater purpose. Just as with the oak sliver, the thorn at first was Paul's whole focus. We naturally look only to our most painful point, not the whole board.

Of course, the natural instinct is to take the sliver out. Paul asked for this three times, likely over an extended period of prayer. But God turned Paul's request around in a remarkable way: "But He said to me, 'My grace is sufficient for you, for My power is made perfect in weakness.' Therefore I will boast all the more gladly of my weakness, so that the power of Christ may rest upon me" (2 Corinthians 12:9). How galling for Satan to see his thorn turned for the glory of God! The answer wasn't to reject the thorn, for that might have merely sent another thorn after it. The key was carrying the board along with the Father. If I had one sliver, Dad had more. When I carried my few inches, Dad carried the board. Now when you and I have a spiritual sliver, remember the Father's Son, who carried the cross and bore the nails. God's power filled Paul's weakness through the gift of the thorn.

The thorn in the flesh was itself a fixed instrument. A similar but more agile attack came with the serpents of Numbers 21. Here we see an even more dramatic example of how God turned the illness into the cure. The people of Israel complained again of the tedious journey through the sand and the lack of food besides manna. In judgment, God sent fiery serpents to the people so that those who were bitten died. The people came in repentance to Moses, asking that he pray for God to remove the serpents. This is the essence of our ordinary cure. We cure with distance. Remove the serpents, and we'll be well.

But God instructed Moses to make a bronze serpent, place it on a pole, and call all those who were bitten to look upon it and live. Instead of putting distance between the people and the serpents, God cured the people by bringing this one serpent near. Come near, not far. Look at the serpent, not away from it. The cure lies in the illness itself.

As we know, this incident becomes the foundation for Jesus' own work on the cross. In John 3:14–15, Jesus says, "And as Moses lifted up the serpent in the wilderness, so must the Son of Man be lifted up, that whoever believes in Him may have eternal life." Of all the animals with which to be associated, hasn't Jesus chosen the last one we expect? The serpent is the ancient foe of Genesis 3, the cause of the curse. The serpent is the instrument of judgment in Numbers 21. Surely, God could use any other creature as His likeness. The lion, the eagle, and even the industrious ant come to mind. But God cures through the illness, so the serpent is the sign of healing. God claims all His creation as His own so that even the serpent still serves Him. God twists the serpent, turning him from death to life. From the never-living serpent came healing; from the living Son of God who chose to die comes eternal life.

The people were drawn to the serpent to live. We put the image of the Son of God dying on the cross on the wall opposite dying men. Pointing to Him who died, we say, "Look, there is your hope." Nearness to death, His death, becomes the solution for our approaching death. In other biblical moments, the same tension exists. We naturally seek distance as our cure, but God brings the problem inescapably near to us as the answer.

The Passover and its ultimate expression in the Lord's Supper work this way. The essence of the Passover of Exodus 12 was that God was going to kill the firstborn of all the Egyptians but would pass over the people of Israel whose homes were marked by the blood of the sacrificial lamb. Imagine being the firstborn in the family that night. How close to the door would you sit? As far away as possible! The relief of Passover night was that God had, in fact, passed over you.

> From the never-living serpent came healing; from the living Son of God who chose to die comes eternal life.

The Lord's Supper is the ultimate expression of Passover. The Supper fulfills the Passover because Jesus instituted it on Passover night, but also because the Supper echoes the Passover themes of protection through the blood of the Lamb and by the death of the firstborn Son of God. But the fundamental answer is changed. In the Passover night of Exodus 12, distance was the solution. God stayed outside the house marked by the blood. If the Passover's safety was in the distance of a few feet, God outside the door and we safely on the other side, then wouldn't the ultimate Passover be even more distant? Lord, don't miss me by a few feet, but be as east is from the west, as heaven is high above the earth. We find security in our separation because we fear God's nearness.

But the Lord's Supper gives us the true solution when Jesus says simply, "Take, eat; this is My body" (Matthew 26:26). Our peace with God comes with His presence, not His distance. He collapses our distance as He destroys our fears. He comes not to destroy us because He has Himself already died to make this meal. He brings this bread and wine, body and blood, to us and within us so that we are never passed over but are one with Him in forgiveness. The nearness of God, which was once our fear, has now become our peace.

WOULD THREE DAYS BE ENOUGH?
MAYBE IF IT RAINED.

So far we have had our Mother's Day corsage from five-year-old Amy. Mom wore the corsage on Mother's Day, but do you expect her to wear it again next Sunday? No, once is fine. It can go on the shelf in the family room, and if Amy asks if she is going to wear it again, Mom can say she doesn't want to wear it out.

But what if we're dealing with a new problem. Let's say you have a ten-year-old boy who loves camping—tent camping, sleeping right on the ground. In his vision, there are no cots, no air mattresses, just the sleeping bag on the tent floor. He wants to cook everything over a fire. No trusty Coleman propane stove that will burn in a monsoon. No, over the fire. Oh, and he doesn't want to drive to the campsite. He wants to hike in, carrying all the gear. This brings two questions: Has he ever done this? Do you want to be a part of this?

> Our peace with God comes with His presence, not His distance.

No, on both counts. As far as any camping experience goes, he went overnight once this summer in the backyard at his friend's house. They made it through most of the night before retreating back inside. But your son is sure that a real camping trip miles from any possible escape will be different. (You're sure he's right on that one. It will be different.) Somehow he's found every camping website on the internet, read every camping book in his school library, and wandered down the camping aisle on every visit to Walmart.

You're a good parent. You've gone along with so many of his interests, and you have the unused tennis rackets, hockey sticks, and empty baseball-card binders to show for it. You just don't want to go camping. But it seems the more you bring up cold, rain, flies, and bears, the more determined he is. So maybe, you think, the illness could be the cure. Instead of avoiding camping, dive in deep. Get your brother-in-law who loves to camp to take him on the very trip he dreams of. Three days, two nights, one tent, no cots, no air mattresses, no Coleman stove. Just a fire and a single pan to cook with. Go early in June in the far north woods when it is still in the forties in the morning. Maybe this deep dive into camping will be the cure.

That's the next step for us also. So far, we've seen the illness transformed to become the cure. We've taken the many existing serpents and reduced them to one bronze serpent. We've taken the comfortable distance of Passover and shrunk it to the nearness of the Supper. But what if making the illness into the cure also involves increasing the problem? What if the measure of the increase is the measure of its cure?

For example, the problem increased with the widow's oil in 2 Kings 4. The widow came to Elijah asking for advice. Her debts were so large that her sons were about to be sold into slavery. Elijah asked what she had in the house. Only a jar of oil, she answered. So Elijah told her to gather every jar from every neighbor she could find. What an answer! She had an empty house with empty cupboards and only empty jars. Emptiness was the problem. And his solution was to increase the emptiness. Gather every empty jar you could find. Then pour from the jar of oil into these jars. Each new jar was filled until every jar was topped off, and she sold the jars of oil to pay off her debts. How satisfying and yet sad when she said to her son, "'Bring me another vessel.' And he said to her, 'There is not another'" (2 Kings 4:6). The measure of her emptiness became the measure of her answer. The daring to not only face the problem but to increase it set the size of the miracle. I wonder if she and her boys didn't ask themselves when it was all done, "Why did we ever stop gathering jars?" If only they had increased the problem, the cure would have been all the greater.

God increased the problem to bring about the cure in an even greater way in Jesus' trial and final sentence. Pilate was in a terrible vise during Jesus' trial. Matthew 27:11–23 describes the trial before Pilate. Jesus, after affirming He was the King of the Jews, then said nothing. Pilate was astonished that Jesus responded to not even a single charge (Matthew 27:14). Pilate's wife warned Pilate to have nothing to do with this innocent man. Pilate veered to the other extreme and found the worst criminal, Barabbas, expecting the crowd to choose the

> The measure of her emptiness became the measure of her answer.

innocent Jesus to be freed. Yet in the end, Pilate had to point to Jesus and ask, "What evil has He done?" (Matthew 27:23). Pilate could not find one thing wrong. And so an innocent man was crucified. Here, Pilate, is your crime! We should condemn the injustice and point out Jesus' perfection. Jesus should be the one who brings life, not the one pressed toward death.

But here the cure comes not by avoiding the evil but by compounding it. The lasting image of Jesus on the cross, lifted up like the serpent on Moses' staff, is one of multiplied sin, our sin, put to death. Now we rush forward to the cross, but not to scold the executioners for their mistakes. We come to the cross with all the reasons for His death. The cure is not in His perfect life alone but in His willingness to receive every sin from every soul. Pilate could not find a single thing wrong with Jesus. But we find every wrong we've ever done hung upon Him as He fills our place on the cross. The widow brought empty jars waiting to be filled. We bring lives filled with sin needing to be emptied. The cure is this: "For our sake He made Him to be sin who knew no sin, so that in Him we might become the righteousness of God" (2 Corinthians 5:21).

God cured us by multiplying the sins charged against His Son. The cross was an evil that innocence should flee. But God cured the world through that injustice, likely leaving the angels in silent wonder. Let the evil come, let all sins gather, and let all charges lie against Him. Have the Father say not one word for His Son.

Let the illness grow until it takes in the whole world. Then it will become the cure for all when it lies upon the cross.

IT'S TIME FOR PATIENCE

The summer between seventh and eighth grade, I fell off a tractor on our farm. I was hurrying to get down from our Farmall Super H to hook up a hay wagon and get quickly back to the field where Dad was baling hay. I slipped, missed the step on the draw-bar, and tore my left shin open to the bone. Mom and Dad drove me to the clinic at Wadena, where I was stitched up and sent home on crutches.

For the next six weeks of summer, I was on crutches. I couldn't work in the barn or shop, but I could clean strawberries and snap beans for Mom, chores almost as dull as picking rocks. What saved that summer was my Aunt Mae. Mae, who lived in Minneapolis, brought over a complete hardbound set of Mark Twain's books for me. A well-to-do family was about to throw them away, and Mae rescued them for me. I read every one of them and still have them in the bookcase in our family room, one shelf below Nicole's green pot. Mark Twain made such an impression on me that I became an English major in college. I suppose much of the writing of this book goes back to a love of reading, especially Mark Twain. That lost, long summer stretched into a lifetime of books.

So far, our examples have largely been instant examples of the illness becoming the cure. The single day with the serpents, the day of gathering jars, and the short hours of Jesus' trial have all taken place quickly and shown us the cure. All those cures came in less than a day. But what if the illness is changed into a long, patient cure so that the illness, which would have been fatal in a moment, is transformed into a lasting solution? Then we have the patience that we expect of God.

Moses' early life is an example of the sort of patience that turns the illness into the cure. Exodus begins by relating the cruel verdict of Pharaoh: "Every son that is born to the Hebrews you shall cast into the Nile" (Exodus 1:22). Clearly for an Israelite mother of a son, the Nile and Pharaoh are the center of evil. Moses' mother gives birth to him and hides him for three months until there is no more hiding. Where to go? Our normal reaction would be the one Moses takes forty years later: flee to the desert. Put as much distance as possible between yourself and the problem.

But Moses' mother goes to the center of evil, the river Nile where Pharaoh's daughter was bathing. Pharaoh's daughter sees Moses in his small basket floating among the reeds and retrieves him. She has surprising pity on the boy, whom she knows is one of the condemned Israelite children. But rather than drowning him as commanded by her father, she draws him from the water to be raised within Pharaoh's household.

What a conversion of evil into the cure. For the next forty years, Moses is a member of the very household that had condemned him to death. How Moses might have gone back to that same spot at the Nile where he was found and marveled at the place where he was rescued. There he should have died, but there he was given these decades of life. How that might have been also a wonder to the other Israelites. While they are in slavery, Moses lives in the household of Pharaoh. What natural resentment might have come against him? He is no different, no better than any other Israelite, and yet, look, there he is, safe and well, while they're slaves.

If you heard an outburst of anger and resentment like that, wouldn't you want to say just a word? Listen to the slaves condemn Moses for all his advantages. He's the problem, with his life in Pharaoh's home! Come to these men and say, "You know, the illness will become the cure. The very one you despise with all his advantages will be the one who not only rescues you from slavery but also will destroy the very household of Pharaoh." Would they believe it? I doubt they could. What good would ever come from the household of Pharaoh? But that is the wonder of Moses' life.

THIS ROAD GOES NOWHERE

Six Mile Road goes nowhere except straight into a grove of trees. If you are traveling south on Six Mile, just five miles south of our house, your GPS will show that the road goes straight ahead when you come to the Sheboygan/Ozaukee county line. But look, Six Mile Road goes nowhere. The view over your hood shows only trees.

The surveyors for the two counties must have had quite an argument as to which one was right. When they met at the county line, they were off from each other by thirty-nine feet, two inches. Six Mile Road, which is only twenty-one feet wide in itself, dead ends at County K, so you have to turn left, go thirty-nine feet, and turn right in order to go ahead.

The road looks to go nowhere, but the GPS says you can keep going straight. Squint your eyes to what's only right ahead and it's hopeless. But the GPS says there's a road there. Our theme is much the same. Our journey through illness says the problem is a dead end. There's no cure and no hope. Stop, turn, and go back if you can, but you can't go forward. But God says there is a way forward. The way forward may seem to be full of thick trees, but take a wider view. What if God did even more than simply have us turn thirty-nine feet and keep going? What if God said that the tree right ahead of you, the one that seems your end, is really the cure? The tree of the cross that stands before us seems as foolishness for us. But aim straight for it; that's God's path. God's plan for each of us takes us through the cross, through what seems to be the problem itself to find the road to life on the other side.

CHARCOAL CAKE

In the story of Moses, we have two contrasting images of Pharaoh and his household. Pharaoh's own ruthless edict that all the

Israelite boys be drowned is simply horrible. But then we have Pharaoh's daughter taking Moses in, knowing that he was an Israelite baby. With that, we might have to say that at least she wasn't anything like her father. It depends on how you see the family.

It's a bit like burnt toast. Is it really burnt? I would guess that we've all grown up with toast that has been, if not burnt, then very, very well done. There's that smell, and the smoke alarm quivers on the edge of beeping. Pop that toast out and let it hit your plate. It clinks. Is the toast burnt? Depends on whom you ask. The ten-year-old says, "It's burnt again. Look, it's all black." Mom says, "It's not burnt. It's just well done." But if you keep on complaining, she has the fix. She hands you a butter knife and says, "If it bothers you so much, here, just scrape it off." The sound of your childhood breakfasts was the sound of that knife scraping black toast.

Scrape down a bit, and the toast gets lighter. Be careful and do the other side, but don't wear all the way through the toast. Put on the jam and eat away. But what did you do with the charcoal you scraped off? Even your mother who insisted that the toast wasn't burnt didn't save the charcoal, did she? She never said, "Save that. I'm making charcoal cake this afternoon."

But God saved it and made it the defining ingredient in His most famous recipe. Hershey's chocolate cake takes one and a third cup of their cocoa to make a fantastic cake. God took the rejected charcoal of a desperate life to make the most famous life in the New Testament. That which the Church would have gladly thrown out, and impatiently expected God to discard, was remade into the life of St. Paul.

Consider Paul as perhaps the ultimate example of God curing with the illness itself. Here we see God's enduring patience in the darkest times of Paul's life, even during his persecution of Christians. Then God confronts Paul, scrapes away his past, and yet saves that persecution to become the key ingredient of Paul's new life. All this allows Paul to make the most dramatic statement of his own transformed life and to point out that what God had done with him was only a small reflection of what He had done with His own Son.

Paul as the murdering Pharisee Saul was certainly the illness plaguing the Early Christian Church. His campaign to find and destroy members of the Church as recorded in Acts 9 must have prompted many prayers that God would remove him from the world. But instead of taking the illness away, God transformed Paul and placed him in the very center of the Early Church. Instead of his name being the curse of death, Paul's words have been a ringing statement of faith, hope, and love centered on Jesus alone.

> The sound of your childhood breakfasts was the sound of that knife scraping black toast.

After three days of fearful darkness, Paul's conversion came through the enlightenment of Baptism and recovery of his sight. Immediately, he began preaching the Gospel, much to people's astonishment. This statement about Paul captures our illness/cure theme: "He who used to persecute us is now preaching the faith he once tried to destroy" (Galatians 1:23). Paul looked over his former life of persecution and harnessed that as an example for all Christians. He acknowledged that he was the worst of sinners, which had this purpose: "But I received mercy for this reason, that in me, as the foremost, Jesus Christ might display His perfect patience as an example to those who were to believe in Him for eternal life" (1 Timothy 1:16). Paul became the ultimate example of the cure coming through the illness itself.

Since Paul could see the usefulness of his own errors, he used that in his preaching. In Athens, Paul encountered the many altars to the various Greek gods, gods so many that there was even a statue to the unknown god. Instead of denouncing this as polytheistic foolishness, Paul called the Athenians very religious people. "What therefore you worship as unknown, this I proclaim to you" (Acts 17:23). Paul used that altar as a doorway to the one true God the Athenians did not yet know but which they in a vacuum had tried to worship. Their unlabeled door could become the path of discovery.

Paul turned the foolishness of the Athenians into wisdom. Perhaps Paul's strongest statement of our theme came with a similar description of the Gospel message of the cross in 1 Corinthians 1. Paul notes that the words of the cross are foolishness and weakness to both Jews and Gentiles. But Paul had only one message: "But we preach Christ crucified, a stumbling block to Jews and folly to Gentiles, but to those who are called, both Jews and Greeks, Christ the power of God and the wisdom of God" (1 Corinthians 1:23–24). The futility of the cross endures as a power that cannot be toppled and a wisdom that cannot be faulted.

More Than Day-Old Bread and Bread Pudding

My mother never made charcoal cake from the scrapings of burnt toast. But we did have a lot of bread pudding made from old bread. We had banana bread from bananas that were definitely past eating. The genius of these recipes is that they don't replace the ingredients that are too old. They use them just as they are, too old and too black.

Making banana bread takes patience and creativity. Banana bread isn't instant food. Impatience won't age the bananas any faster. Leave them alone and don't worry about those dark spots. Tell your five-year-old, "Trust me. They're turning out just right for our bread." Your five-year-old looks at that black-spotted banana and says, "I would never eat that." Then tell her, "You're right, you wouldn't. But you'll be amazed at the bread it'll make."

Isn't that much the conversation we have with God over this theme? Our impatience demands an instant, perfect answer to the illnesses we face. We want distance from our problems, not nearness. We want to sweep our troubles off the counter, not leave them to ripen. But with this theme, God shows the two qualities we so often lack, patience and a creative turn.

> The futility of the cross endures as a power that cannot be toppled and a wisdom that cannot be faulted.

Patience sometimes means evil will continue for a time. Paul threatened Christians for months, maybe years. The widow gathered more empty jars for a house that was already empty. This baffles us when we expect God to show an immediate, obvious answer to demonstrate His power. But God's patience waits. Perhaps you are in the middle of that waiting time. You are feeling the length of a long night, such as the one Psalm 30:5 mentions: "Weeping may tarry for the night, but joy comes with the morning." It is a long, questioning night in which darkness seems only to increase.

But God's timing matches His creativity. It isn't merely that God waits out evil and sees that it exhausts itself. Instead, God creatively uses the evil. Paul's record as the worst sinner makes him the spokesperson for all who hope for God's mercy. The false charges against Jesus aren't cleared away but are the needed tools that deliver Him to the cross. The serpents, if they could talk, would have hissed in anger that a bronze model of themselves healed those bitten. Whoever invented banana bread was one bold, creative woman. But maybe she stumbled onto the recipe by luck and necessity. Even more so, God uses the evil intentionally to bring the good He desires. By the sins of the world, He demonstrates His love through the cross. God cures with the illness itself.

"MY SONG IS LOVE UNKNOWN"

The essence of the Gospel is that God uses Jesus' death to cure the world. Lenten hymns especially capture this theme. One of the most beautiful is "My Song Is Love Unknown" (*LSB* 430). The contrast of our theme comes immediately in stanza 1.

> My song is love unknown,
>> My Savior's love to me,
> Love to the loveless shown
>> That they might lovely be.
> Oh, who am I
>> That for my sake
>> My Lord should take
> Frail flesh and die?

His love given to the loveless brings Him to death but brings the love of God to those who hate Him. The hymn summarizes His love and miracles, His gifts that were returned with hatred. Stanza 5 shows the final Good Friday moments when Barabbas is released but Jesus is condemned:

> They rise and needs will have
>> My dear Lord made away;
> A murderer they save,
>> The Prince of Life they slay.
> Yet cheerful He
>> To suff'ring goes
>> That He His foes
> From thence might free.

It's all wrong to release the guilty and kill the innocent. But that is the injustice that justifies the world, the death that brings life, the illness that becomes the cure.

DISCUSSION QUESTIONS

1. The chapter began by describing a Mother's Day corsage of knotted yarn. What Mother's Day or Father's Day gifts did you make or what gifts like that have you received? How perfect was the design and artwork? And yet, what response were you hoping to receive when you gave it?

2. How does God use what is flawed to bring out His love and grace? When has God preserved our corsage of knots to show His relationship with us?

3. We noted that we generally want an immediate cure with distance, with opposites. When is that so for you? For example, consider what you want to have happen when you have a cold, your car's "check engine" light has come on, or you've received four new bills?

4. How does God value patience and creativity in His use of the evil in our lives so that the evil becomes the foundation of the cure?

5. We used several biblical examples of the illness becoming the cure. Here is one we didn't discuss: Joseph angered his brothers by telling them of his dreams in Genesis 37. What terrible "illness" comes to Joseph because of the dreams? However, how do dreams provide the cure for Joseph in Genesis 40 and 41?

6. We discussed the widow's oil in 2 Kings 4 as a prime example of this theme. How difficult would it have been to be the widow and her sons, gathering nothing but empty jars? Would you have quit early from gathering, or would you have gone on to the very last house possible?

7. The ultimate example of this theme is the cross on which Jesus is lifted up, in the likeness of the bronze serpent. How surprising is it that Jesus would make this comparison between Himself and the serpent, given the work of the serpent in Genesis 3? Why would God do this and not compare Himself here with another animal such as a lion, a bear, or an eagle?

CHAPTER 8

PERFECTION WELCOMES FAILURE

My friends who are nurses tell me that the following story could actually happen. Imagine a woman named Sarah has just started her first job as a nurse. She's a float pool nurse working on the OB unit, second shift, just hoping to avoid any big mistakes. So far, she's done all right because no one has left her on her own. Which is good considering that Katarina Reichart, Sarah's supervising nurse, is truly frightening. She's a full six feet of fearsome. She stares the world down over her half-lens glasses. Her uniform, even after a full shift, is starched stiff. She doesn't just know the policy and procedure manual; she wrote it herself on two stone tablets. The doctors need her permission before they can go home. When she steps onto the hospital floor, everyone either snaps to attention or flees into a room.

Then Sarah's story takes a turn, but honest, she didn't know. Sarah spent her whole shift taking care of every mother on the floor. She checked them over and over, and they were fine. At the end of the shift, Sarah went to the nurses' station to fill out the change of shift report. Then it hits her. She never checked on the babies. She was sure someone else was in charge of the babies and she only had the mothers. But no, she had both. Except she never checked on the babies. On the report, under the column for assessments of the babies, she's got nothing.

Now imagine Sarah hears the approaching steps of Nurse Reichart. She senses a disturbance in her ordered world. The look on Sarah's face is a dead giveaway. What should she do? Run up to Nurse Reichart and say, "You'll never believe what I just did!" Of course not. Sarah would want to duck, cover, hide, or just run, but she definitely wouldn't go toward her boss. There's no way to spin this. Sarah messed up in the worst way, and Nurse Reichart would be the last person she'd want to see.

Unless Nurse Reichart would be God. Then Sarah would strangely run toward her. That is our seventh theme, "Perfection Welcomes Failure." This theme deals with the extremes of perfection and failure. Small errors get swept under the rug, hoping to be hidden. Little mistakes need only small excuses. But when we are truly guilty and there is no way out, then we are drawn to God's perfection. When perfection is only Nurse Reichart, we might try to hide and escape to our car. But when we face God's perfection, we are oddly drawn toward Him.

This Takes Us to the Limit

In my story of the nurse, my nursing friends calmed me by saying that all the babies were fine. The mothers all had the babies with them in their rooms and were feeding and changing them. So take a deep breath. The babies were okay, even if they weren't actually assessed. It was a mistake, but not a huge one.

Small mistakes let us avoid perfection. Only truly huge mistakes drive us to face absolute perfection. We're not going to admit to being truly guilty if it's something that can be explained or excused. We'll hide under the covers of denial and deflection. We'll sidestep perfection's approach by pointing out others worse than ourselves. There are several biblical examples of this, beginning with the Garden of Eden. Adam and Eve heard God coming and hid in their sin, then blamed God and each other. We do the same thing. We hear God coming, and we either have our explanations ready—"No one told me to check on the babies"—or we bolt for the door.

Only truly horrendous mistakes drive us to perfection. It's a bit like getting your car out of the snow. Image you get stuck in five or six inches of snow. You drive until the tires give out and start spinning. There's a bank built up in front of your tires that you need to get through and another bank built up behind your tires from your spinning. How do you get through? Get the car moving back and forth, little by little, shifting the transmission from drive to reverse and back to drive. Each time you rock the car, it goes a little farther. Finally, get it reared back all the way and drop it into drive, and you'll make it.

We'll hide under the covers of denial and deflection.

A little backward movement will get you nowhere. Only when you go all the way back, as far as you can possibly go, are you going to go forward. You only go forward when you go all the way back. So only when we stop our small reversals are we going to go forward to God's perfection. Only those who step the furthest back from excuses are going to be nearest to God. Paul admitted he was the worst of sinners and yet found that this was the path to God's righteousness (1 Timothy 1:13–16). Those imagining themselves holy continue in their sins, while those who admit that they are the worst are justified.

BE A BOOMERANG, NOT A SPEAR

In this theme, we'll first watch those who know only a little of themselves and God. We will find that often those who have a limited grasp of their sin are the farthest from God. They fly a straight course that leads them only farther away from God. This self-induced spiritual deception can be either from a single sin or a lifelong folly. In their minds, people often excuse the single sin by pointing out that it happened only once. Or they will contrast their sin with someone else's worse sin. The lifelong pattern of sin is more difficult to dismiss, but again, people can construct a holiness of their own imagination when they compare their lives with others. We can be the same way. When we have little knowledge of sin, especially our own sin, we can deceive ourselves into thinking we can remain at arm's length from God. Perhaps we'll be remembered as not the worst person in the world, not the best, but not worth investigating. Oh, if Nurse Reichart would only come along and say, "Everything went well today? I'm sure it did." If you were Sarah, wouldn't it be tempting to say, "Uhh, sure. Everyone's fine." Then leave as fast as deception allows. Fly away down the shortest hall you can find and burst through an exit door.

> You only go forward when you go all the way back.

But real spiritual truth is a boomerang. A simple arrow or spear flies away, and the longer it flies, the farther it goes. However, in the main portion of this chapter, we'll survey those biblical times when there was seemingly no escape. The full weight of both our human sin and God's righteousness came upon men and women who found their only hope in the just God they had been avoiding. What a wonder that, in desperation, they returned to the very God they formerly fled.

I would never claim to understand boomerangs even if I were to read the whole Wikipedia article on them. I think I'm safe to say, however, that a key difference between a spear and a boomerang is that the boomerang has two roughly equal arms while the spear is single-bodied. We're spears by spiritual nature, but we're intended to become boomerangs. The single-focus of the spear flies on its own straight course, and once that course begins, it will only go farther away. Left to ourselves, we are launched from conception in sin on that straight course away from God. Our solitary focus on ourselves will only leave us farther from Him.

But the boomerang returns to its origin because of two equal arms. When our arm of failure is matched by an equal arm of God's perfection, we fly back to Him. Knowledge of His holiness is not a flight-ending burden as we might imagine. Knowledge of God is the balance to a truthful recognition of our sin. Instead of these two being impossible opposites, they join to bring us back to God.

> We're spears by spiritual nature, but we're intended to become boomerangs.

David flees God's righteousness when pursuing Bathsheba and killing Uriah. But when Nathan's simple story about the lost lamb convicts David, David returns to God with the words of Psalm 51, crying out for a clean heart and a new spirit. David was on a flight away from God, but God turned David around by balancing David's utter sinfulness with God's perfect holiness. So let's begin this journey. First, we'll fly from God in fear and denial. But when God's absolute perfection is joined to our absolute failure, we'll fly home again to Him.

Clinicals Were Never like This

Let's return to our friend Sarah and her horrifying moment with Nurse Reichart. She makes a fast break down the hall and evades the full scrutiny of Nurse Reichart, who would ask how she could possibly spend a whole shift and never check on the babies. How could she possibly think that assessing the babies wasn't her job?

Well, our nurse friend has an answer. She never had to do that when she was a graduate nurse working on the OB unit in Engelstead Memorial Hospital. During all those shifts at Engelstead, no one ever expected her to do both. It was mothers or babies but never both. So of course, it's not her fault. Someone should have told her. That would be her consolation as she dashes down the hall, wondering if bursting through the emergency exit door would be justified at this moment.

That is the momentum for our first flight away from God. It comes straight from Adam and Eve in Genesis 3. After Adam and Eve ate the forbidden fruit, they hid from God. I suspect they would have fled if they could. In their newfound sinfulness, Adam and Eve were not attracted to God's absolute perfection. Instead, their sin left them paralyzed with guilt. But when God found them, they had the first excuse for their distance: they blamed someone else. Adam said, "The woman whom You gave to be with me, she gave me fruit of the tree, and I ate" (Genesis 3:12). Of course, Eve distanced herself from both Adam and God by saying, "The serpent deceived me, and I ate" (v. 13). Life in perfect Eden was broken into three jagged islands. Adam and Eve separated themselves from God and from each other. This separation was highlighted when Adam and Eve were driven east out of the garden, while an angel with a flaming sword guarded against their return (v. 24).

If Eden's perfection was shattered by this single sin, how much is the already-broken world shaken by our continued sins. When we blame God, we further distance ourselves from God and one another. Jonah is an example of trying to put literal distance between ourselves and God. When God first told Jonah His plan for him to preach to Nineveh, Jonah lived out most dramatically the separation of sin. He fled in the opposite direction, sailing west to Tarshish. While we don't have Jonah's thoughts written down as directly as we have the thoughts of Adam and Eve, we can imagine that Jonah firmly blamed God too. How could God possibly expect him to go to his enemies in Nineveh? It would be suicide for him, a Jew, to go to Nineveh. So in response, Jonah fled in the opposite direction from God's presence and plans.

Though the sin can be single, the direction it sets is clearly away from God. That spear in flight has no intention of turning around. Its only hope is that distance from God will somehow protect it. We might dimly remember the words of Psalm 139, but we deny those words by our fleeing feet. David can say with all spiritual truth and reason: "Where shall I go from Your Spirit? Or where shall I flee from Your presence? If I ascend to heaven, You are there! If I make my bed in Sheol, You are there!" (Psalm 139:7–8). We know all this is true, but it doesn't stop us from escaping. We flee away as a quivering spear, shaken by our guilt, but flying away still. The only mark left behind is the echo of our defense, "It's not my fault!"

You Think You've Got Problems?

Our friend Sarah is almost certainly running away alone. She might even be glad of company in her misery. Imagine her dashing into the stairwell, straight into another nurse also on the run. One of them is bound to ask, "So what did you do?" Maybe she forgot to give out some medication or she lost her patience with the most demanding patient ever. No matter what the new story is, Sarah would say, "That's nothing. Lemme tell you what I did." Compare yourself with others, and you can still feel alone.

So also the distance we gain by blaming God leads naturally to a distance from one another. If it is not enough to look up and blame God, we can always look horizontally to blame others. The sideways glance can be either one of blame or of comparison. Either way, our isolation grows.

The distance from one another is perfectly seen in the two men going to the temple to pray (Luke 18:9–14). Jesus describes the isolation of the Pharisee as he goes forward, praying about his competitive perfection. "God, I thank You that I am not like other men, extortioners, unjust, adulterers, or even like this tax collector. I fast twice a week; I give tithes of all that I get" (Luke 18:11–12). I suspect that the list went on considerably from there. The volume of his speaking must have been just right: quiet enough to have a veneer of piety but loud enough for others to hear. After an opening word to God, he speaks only of his idol—himself. Unlike the tax collector, the Pharisee went home without God's justification. Instead, he went home with self-satisfaction, which he had always had, and maybe he picked up a grudging "Well, good for you" from others who listened.

When we compare our sins with others, we might imagine that we're flying ahead of everyone else. But that doesn't mean we are flying to God, merely that we think we are somehow higher and faster than others. We can always create a contest that we're certain to win. You can run all winter on a treadmill in your exercise room. The temperature will be a perfect 60 degrees, no wind, and the treadmill can be set dead flat, zero incline. You can run fantastic times. Compare your times to someone who runs outdoors all winter, in wind, cold, snow, and sleet, uphill and down— you'll win every comparison. But why are you running? To run the Boston Marathon in April? Then we can only wish you luck. Boston's famous course is relentlessly hilly, and the weather can be a bone-chilling upper 30s with sleet or 88 degrees under a shadeless sun. It's nearly a guarantee that the wind will be in your face for much of the race. Those miles on the treadmill are nothing like the hills of Boston. At some point, you'll stand at the foot of yet another towering hill, with a twenty-mile-an-hour wind in your face, and you'll admit you were never prepared for this. You won the treadmill race, but Boston is something else.

> We flee away as a quivering spear, shaken by our guilt, but flying away still.

So the Pharisee was racing only himself, setting the rules, and calling out the score. His prayer sounded like success, but his race was taking him only farther from God. When he would meet God, he would be as unprepared as the rich fool who gathered his wealth and imagined that with full barns he could eat, drink, and be merry. But God warned this thoughtless man, "Fool! This night your soul is required of you, and the things you have prepared, whose will they be? So is the one who lays up treasure for himself and is not rich toward God" (Luke 12:20–21). Whether one is winning the comparison of wealth or self-directed piety, the result will be a poverty toward God with no currency fit to pay for an eternal soul.

It Can Get Tight in the Corners

The Pharisee saw himself far out in front of the tax collector. The rich fool with his evening of rich food and easy thoughts was coasting to the finish. But there is another mind-set that can lead away from God's perfection. This is when the race is still going on. Then the corners get awfully tight.

A marathon of 25,000 to 40,000 people can get very crowded. The organizers do their best to spread people out and have you run with people of similar speed. Despite that, you still have thousands of competitive people wedged together, all aiming to take the shortest line around every corner. You can say, "Be patient, it's a long race." Say that if you want, but many race each corner as though it's their last. There's no time for patience when they're seeking the perfect pace right now.

That spirit also drives people from God's nearness and perfection. We'd rather grasp something immediately; we have no time for God's patience. David and Bathsheba are a perfect example of this and likely also the first category—distance by blaming others. David wanted what he didn't have, at least what he didn't have yet. We know the sad story of how David saw Bathsheba and brought her to the palace, which resulted in a child, and how David plotted against Uriah, which resulted in Uriah's death. Finally, David and Bathsheba marry, and the child is born. But what a cloud this greedy rush must have brought. Was there any joy in their wedding? Was there any thanksgiving in the birth of their son? These moments are gifts that often turn people toward God in thanks. But we can imagine no thanks between David and Bathsheba but perhaps the very fault-finding that marked Adam and Eve. David was impatient and likely blamed others. He was an arrow flying straight away from God.

What a sad reversal of patience and perfection in David and Bathsheba. After God turned David through the self-condemning story of the lamb that the rich man selfishly took (2 Samuel 12:1–7), Nathan then reminded David that God had given him the kingship, the palace, his wives, and all else that came with the kingship. "And if this were too little, I would add to you as much more" (2 Samuel 12:8). This was the perfection of God's plan, but David had no patience for it. God's generosity appears boundless but it will not be hurried. David's impatient grasp snatched the gift from God's hand and raced away. The perfection of God's plan was lost in the impatience of the moment.

In these three ways of blame, competition, and greed, we can fly away from God's perfection. The sin itself may be as single as eating the fruit of the tree in Eden or as tangled as the multiple sins of David. Regardless, it is sin, which either seeks distance from God or imagines that God has joined us on our self-determined path. Only a seeking, patient, and all-knowing God can collapse that distance so that ultimate perfection attracts even complete failures.

> The perfection of God's plan was lost in the impatience of the moment.

You're on My Unit Now

When we left Sarah, she had just seen Nurse Reichart coming and had dashed off to safety. But let's change that a bit. Sarah is concentrating on the change of shift form. She has just filled in the assessment of the mothers when she realizes that she is expected to assess the babies. The empty space on the form is nothing compared to the chasm of dread she feels inside. At that moment, Nurse Reichart appears at her elbow. There is no escape. Nurse Reichart sees the empty chart and asks, "How are the babies?" Sarah's flushed face, her stammered "Ahh, umm," and the rush of her hand to cover her throat say it all. Nurse Reichart says, "Did you forget to assess the babies?" How does she know this? Perhaps you imagine her asking this question with a sinister twist on "forget." Saying it that way suggests that forgetting the babies is the last thing anyone even pretending to be a nurse would do. "Surely you didn't forget the babies, did you?"

But what if Nurse Reichart says it differently? What if she lowers her voice so only Sarah can hear? What if she pauses before "forget" and then says it with a gentle question mark behind it?

"Did you forget to assess the babies?" What if she asks the question not as the death sentence to your nursing career but as a reminder of one more thing to do before leaving the unit? What if she then said, "You know, when I was first here, I did a whole shift once without ever checking on the mothers. All I looked at was the babies. Only at the end did it hit me that I was supposed to worry about the moms too. It's hard when you're new. So maybe you'll want to stop in to see the babies one more time before you go. In fact, let's divide them up, you and me, so it doesn't take so long and you can get home."

Did you see this coming? Never, not from Nurse Reichart, the embodiment of nursing perfection. Who ever imagined her as a new nurse, making mistakes? And who ever thought she would tell anyone what she had done?

So what would you do if you were Sarah? Maybe you would admit you never knew you were supposed to check the babies. Nurse Reichart seemed to know that, so there'd be no harm in saying it. Don't blame Engelstead Memorial or anyone else. Just admit it. You could even say, "I feel terrible. How could I be so dumb?" But to that Nurse Reichart would say, "Don't worry. No one else knows, just us." And from that day forward, you would be on Nurse Reichart's unit. At the end of every day's shift, she always asks you with a kind smile, "And how are the babies today?" And with a grateful smile, you say, "They're all doing fine."

Perfection attracts failure when the whole story of perfection is known. Nurse Reichart became perfect in Sarah's eyes because her knowledge was matched by mercy. Perfection draws complete failures to admit what happened and to hope for a new life alongside the perfect one. Sarah would no longer want a transfer off Nurse Reichart's unit. After that day, Sarah would want to stay with her. After all, she's perfect.

I Was Old Once Too

Nurse Reichart made her mistake when she was young, just like Sarah did. That's when mistakes are supposed to happen, though I continue to set new age-group records for mistakes. You're never too old for a new mistake.

This is part of our astonishment over God's perfection. He can relate to the troubles we face, and people even counted Him as a complete failure at the end of His life, seen as a criminal worse than the worst. Yes, He experienced the trials and temptations we face, yet He did so without sinning. Hebrews 4:15–16 sets the stage for us: "For we do not have a high priest who is unable to sympathize with our weaknesses, but one who in every respect has been tempted as we are, yet without sin. Let us then with confidence draw near to the throne of grace, that we may receive mercy and find grace to help in time of need." Here is the center of our theme: God's perfection is both His holiness and, in Christ, His perfect knowledge and experience of all that tempts us. Jesus perfectly endured temptations without sin. When met with that kind of perfection, we might want to run away from Him. How easily He could meet us in our failures and say, "I went through that—and much more—and never fell. What's wrong with you?" From that question, we would flee.

But instead He draws us to Himself by not only knowing the temptation but by standing under the judgment of the sins themselves. Jesus was charged not for a mistake on the first day on the job but at the end of His adult ministry; He stood condemned for the sins of the world. Paul describes the great exchange of righteousness and sin that occurred on the cross: "For our sake He made Him to be sin who knew no sin, so that in Him we might become the righteousness of God" (2 Corinthians 5:21). Forsaken by the Father and crucified under God's judgment, Jesus bore the sin of the world by becoming that sin Himself. No one can explain completely what this passage promises, but by faith we accept this new dimension of Jesus' perfection. He not only perfectly defeated all temptation, but He also completely carried the guilt for all that He did not do. He was perfectly holy and completely condemned. This is the combination that draws sinners to His throne of grace. Hebrews sums it up again: "Therefore He had to be made like His brothers in every respect, so that He might become a merciful and faithful high priest in the service of God, to make propitiation for the sins of the people. For because He Himself has suffered when tempted, He is able to help those who are being tempted" (Hebrews 2:17–18).

YOU GO WHERE YOU ARE LOOKING

It's a truth from driver's education class: you go where you're looking. If you fixate on the pothole, even though you tell yourself not to go there, you'll hit it. Wherever you're looking, that's where you're going. This can be a problem with more than potholes. When you're driving along, almost anything can become your fixation. Watch the cute puppy playing in the yard and soon you've driven up onto the sidewalk. The puppy is thrilled but your passengers, not so much.

Perfection can draw our attention. You're driving along and the perfect sunrise is happening off to your left. Keep checking it, but watch that other lane also. The mountains finally come into view as you drive west toward Denver. Keep looking, but notice that the road finally has a curve.

God's perfection can have the same fascination. Our principle of perfection attracting failure works as we contemplate God's perfection. While there are many chances for us to do this, perhaps one of the best and most concentrated times is when taking the Lord's Supper. We come to the Supper knowing that we have failed, and yet we're invited. Consider Jesus' simple words: "Do this in remembrance of Me" (Luke 22:19). What a moment for perfection and failure to meet. Here we have His very body and blood, broken and shed, yet perfect as His gift to us for eternal life. And in this moment, we can linger with our thoughts lifted from ourselves to Him. Remember Him, His miracles, His parables, His patience, and His power. Here you can be drawn safely toward the One on whom you are focused. Perfection safely attracts failure as we remember Him.

LET'S NOT TALK ABOUT IT

We approach the mystery of how Jesus innocently bore our guilt with silence. It's too deep to understand but too generous to be questioned. Perhaps silence is the language of faith and trust. That captures a famous example of perfection welcoming failure: the prodigal son. In the parable of Luke 15:11–32, Jesus tells us of a younger son who fled home with the premature inheritance. When the money was gone, he came to his senses and returned home. He rehearsed his apology and was hoping to be a servant within his father's house. But his father welcomed him without a single condemning word. The son's apology is cut short by the father's directions. He gave no commands to condemn but orders for the celebration. Bring the robe, the ring, and the shoes. Tell everyone to come for my son is home!

From that moment on, we hear nothing from the son. Perhaps he said little all night. Certainly it was not the time to tell the stories of his days on the road. Wonder-filled silence is the sound when perfect mercy welcomes regretful failure. I wonder if the father and son would have ever talked about all that happened on the road. I doubt it. If either one started, I suspect the other said, "Let's not talk about it. We're home together now." Perfect forgiveness covers all that is said and all that is unsaid.

On the other hand, while the son never finished his apology, another man gave full voice to his concerns, and his approach to God dramatically exemplifies our theme. Perfection didn't merely attract failure; perfection drew failure out of the graveyard.

In Mark 5, the demon-possessed man raced down the hill from the graveyard where he lived to meet Jesus. He fell at Jesus' feet, saying, "What have You to do with me, Jesus, Son of the Most High God? I adjure You by God, do not torment me" (Mark 5:7). We might have imagined that this man, controlled by a legion of demons, would have remained as far from Jesus as possible, retreating into the darkest cavern and tomb. But knowing that the powerful Son of God was there, he raced forward even though the demons knew they might be destroyed. The quiet arrival of the Son of God brought shrieking demons out of the graveyard. Perfection attracts failure on a grand scale.

What a contrast between these two, the prodigal son and the demon-possessed man. Both were living on the edge of death. They could have focused on only their darkness and doom. But they saw beyond that to the Father and the Son. For the prodigal, his hope led him on the long march home. For the demon-possessed man, it was a short dash downhill. For both of them, their journeys were marked by patience and faith to match the perfection of God's mercy. The boy could only walk so fast, and the demon-possessed man had to leave the dark security of the graves. For both, they had to patiently trust that each moment was a step toward rescue. So we might be in the middle of the journey that is God's perfect rescue. Nothing about this day and these steps says divine perfection. Yet, when our utter need seeks His perfect supply, then the rescue has already begun.

It's too deep to understand but too generous to be questioned.

BUT WE DO NEED TO TALK

We ended well with Nurse Reichart the last time we thought of her. She sent Sarah off to do half the babies while she did the rest. She assured Sarah that she would stay with her on her OB unit. Now, the two nurses seem to add another sentence to their private, shared stories at the end of each shift. They whisper a few words to each other and nudge elbows. It's all a mystery to the other nurses. Sarah even begins to look for Nurse Reichart on the floor. No one does this. They look out for her but never actually want to find her. Others ask, "Has anyone seen Nurse Reichart?" But Sarah says, "Has anyone seen Katarina?"

It's all because the two of them have begun to talk. Absolute perfection not only welcomes complete failure but it also begins a conversation. It might be short at first, but it can grow. We have two examples of these extremes. For example, the tax collector's very short conversation with God is perfect. He is the opposite of the Pharisee we discussed earlier from the parable of Luke 18:9–14. While the Pharisee had much to say about himself in competition to others, the tax collector had only one sentence. "God, be merciful to me, a sinner!" (Luke 18:13). But this was enough. Jesus assured His listeners that this man went home justified. We can imagine that the tax collector had much more to say as to the nature of his sin and his complete need for mercy alone. But if the conversation had to be reduced to an essential sentence, this one would do.

On the other hand, David gives us a longer conversation in Psalm 51 to express the meeting of perfection and failure. This was David's response after Nathan uncovered his sin. Isn't it surprising how God used David's moral failure to give us this psalm? We would imagine that this incident would be hushed over. We might also imagine that it would be the perfect setting for us to compare ourselves with David. How easily we could avoid a genuine meeting with God's perfection by focusing on David's sins and then saying, "Well, I certainly never murdered anyone!" But instead Psalm 51 speaks for all of us. David speaks of our complete failure from conception to today, and he blames only himself. But he also knows that God's forgiveness completely scrubs our past clean and renews our heart. Perhaps the words that best show the intersection of perfection and failure are these: "Create in me a clean heart, O God, and renew a right spirit within me. Cast me not away from Your presence, and take not Your Holy Spirit from me. Restore to me the joy of Your salvation, and uphold me with a willing spirit" (Psalm 51:10–12).

Here is the conversation we want with God, the words we need to have when our failure meets His perfection. The wonder is that these are not only the words we wish to say, but they are the promise that God has already made. In Christ, all who believe in Him are new creations and are renewed each day. The new heart that we desire comes with His perfect forgiveness, and we have His own words to share with Him each day.

Would You Help the New Ones?

One day, Nurse Reichart finds Sarah and says, "Sarah, good, I was looking for you. We have a new float pool nurse coming on today. Would you get her started, let her know how we do things here?" What an amazing change in their relationship! Now Sarah is the embodiment of Nurse Reichart's unit, and she gets to tell someone new how it's done. Sarah will be the one to tell the new nurse to check on both the moms and the babies. Sarah remembers how tough things were for her that first day, so she's the perfect person for the job.

Paul was that perfect person for the job in God's plans. Paul embodied rebellion against God up to the moment he was met with blinding light and the accusing words, "Why are you persecuting Me?" (Acts 9:4). Paul's former assurance of perfection in his Pharisee life disappeared. In Philippians 3:4–6, Paul cataloged his former boastings in the flesh, ending with "as to righteousness under the law, blameless" (Philippians 3:6). But this was merely more distance away from God's actual perfection. When Paul was turned on the Damascus road, he arrived at the intersection of perfection and failure.

Paul then understood his true standing with God and the purpose of that past. Much later, in writing to Timothy, Paul described his actual resume with God, one that sounds completely useless. "Though formerly I was a blasphemer, persecutor, and insolent opponent. But I received mercy because I had acted ignorantly in unbelief" (1 Timothy 1:13). Who would want a man who failed so? Paul explained the purpose God saw in him: "Christ Jesus came into the world to save sinners, of whom I am the foremost. But I received mercy for this reason, that in me, as the foremost, Jesus Christ might display His perfect patience as an example to those who were to believe in Him for eternal life" (1 Timothy 1:15–16). Here is why God chose Paul. The intersection of Paul's failure and God's perfection was not a simple stop. That is the crossroad of every Christian. Every Christian walks the road of worst sinner and meets the same astonishing grace.

So there is a purpose for the journey that leads first to dark fear and hopelessness. Whether we are a demon-possessed man doomed to life in the graveyard, the prodigal son starving in a far-off country, or David whose carefully concealed sin has just been brought out into the open, God has patiently endured with our sin in order to come to this intersecting moment. God in His patience does not blindly endure sin. God patiently and creatively turns that sin to the point where it is disarmed before His perfection. Then God's perfection welcomes our sinful failure, draws it surprisingly forward, and hears its cry for mercy. God's

> Every Christian walks the road of worst sinner and meets the same astonishing grace.

mercy creates in us a new heart, a new relationship, and sends us out as living examples of the reclamation that God alone can produce.

"ROCK OF AGES, CLEFT FOR ME"

While many hymns express our theme of perfection welcoming failure, the last two stanzas of "Rock of Ages" (*LSB* 761) say it perfectly. Stanza 3 expresses our sorry condition but also His welcome to each of us. We can hear the cry of Psalm 51 here also as we need the shelter and cleansing only God can provide.

> Nothing in my hand I bring;
> Simply to Thy cross I cling.
> Naked, come to Thee for dress;
> Helpless look to Thee for grace;
> Foul, I to the fountain fly;
> Wash me, Savior, or I die.

The next stanza continues our theme of perfection as God's throne and judgment are described even while we come to the end of life. But our death and His eternity, our frailty and His judgment are not impossible opposites. Instead, they come together here:

> While I draw this fleeting breath,
> When mine eyelids close in death,
> When I soar to worlds unknown,
> See Thee on Thy judgment throne,
> Rock of Ages, cleft for me,
> Let me hide myself in Thee.

With all our failings, flee to the Rock that is opened to us all. Find in His strength your shelter and in His arms a perfect welcome.

Discussion Questions

1. Nurse Reichart is likely more frightening than your first boss or supervisor. Yet you probably have a story of some mistake on that first job. What did you do or fail to do, and how did it turn out when the truth came out?

2. On the other hand, Nurse Reichart isn't nearly frightening enough when compared to the complete holiness of God. Read Job 38, at least verses 1–11. How is God here far more frightening than any supervisor you've faced? Why would God ask Job these impossible questions at this time?

3. The chapter listed three ways we avoid God's perfection: we blame others, compete with or compare ourselves to others, or become impatiently greedy. When God confronts us, why is it our natural reaction to blame others for their role in our failings and perhaps also blame God?

4. The Pharisee in the temple in Luke 18:9–14 exemplified how we compare ourselves with others. In the Pharisee's mind, he was winning a contest of his own making. When have you seen people take pride in winning a competition that they create and they alone can win?

5. Nurse Reichart has a surprising change halfway through the chapter when she helps Sarah check on the babies. Did you expect this of her? Would you trust her after that? When have you found a Nurse Reichart, frightening at the start but eventually a trusted help and even friend?

6. God shows remarkable patience in waiting for our failure to reach a critical point so that we might be changed by His perfection. How might we mistake and even misuse God's patience?

7. David and Paul are examples of how God's perfection welcomes our failure. They became models for all Christians. How have you used your failures as a model for others as Paul spoke of in 1 Timothy 1:13–16?

CHAPTER 9

There's More to Be Found

I've been reading motorcycle magazines since I started riding motorcycles in 1970. My first bike was a used 1967 Yamaha 305, and I've always liked those bikes from 1967 to the early seventies. The best motorcycle magazine back then was *Cycle*, though it sadly went out of business in the early 1990s. I began subscribing to *Cycle* in 1972 and got every issue to its end. I've kept every issue. Recently I discovered that online auctions have *Cycle* for sale from the years I missed, from 1967 to 1972. What a treasure! Just last week I bought twelve issues of *Cycle* from 1967 to 1968. Cost? Ten dollars for all twelve. What a deal! I've never read any of them, so I have hours of enjoyment waiting for me this winter. They are a little musty, so to air them out, they're spread across the seats of the Model T in the garage for now. When are they coming inside the house? Good question. Holly and I are discussing that right now. The answer is this: sometime between soon and never, depending on whom you ask.

But imagine what I have spread on that Model T seat. More of what I love to read and have never read before. You just don't find that every day. Wouldn't it be wonderful if the same were true of the Bible? What if we had a new chapter to read today and a whole new book waiting for us this winter? But there is none. It's unlikely that any new letters from Paul will be found. In fact, John seems to close the door on our hopes when he says, "Now Jesus did many other signs in the presence of the disciples, which are not written in this book; but these are written so that you may believe that Jesus is the Christ, the Son of God, and that by believing you may have life in His name" (John 20:30–31). Whatever we might find would only tell the same truth that has already come:

Jesus is the Son of God, and we have life by His life, death, and resurrection.

Still, it would be exciting to have something new to read. Perhaps we have some of that interest and discovery with the seven themes we've used here. I hope that the seven themes have given you new interest and perspective on familiar Bible stories. Now there are two more ways to expand what is still new in the Bible. First, in this chapter, we'll combine two or three of the themes as they intersect in the same Bible account. You've likely done some of that as you've been reading already. We talked of an event, and you thought of a previous theme and connected that theme with the text we were discussing. So we'll bring these together with several possibilities. Think of us braiding together two or three threads to make something strikingly new.

Second, besides using the seven themes, we'll suggest new themes. You've likely done this also as we've gone along. My list of seven is only my list. Yours is likely much more creative. I'll suggest some possible themes that might ignite your creativity, but don't wait for me. Go ahead in thinking of those repeated patterns of action and thought that you've observed in several biblical accounts. The biblical accounts stay the same, but how we connect them with one another can be new.

The result comes by asking familiar Bible stories a simple, new question: Which of the seven themes is working here? The answer could be more than one, as we'll see in this chapter. Also as you see patterns occur, you can ask another new question: What's connecting these events and people? You can go backward and forward on the contextual river, asking when you have seen this before and when you might see it again. Then you begin to braid the two, three, or four biblical narratives together to make a single theme that includes them all.

I have to admit that the old *Cycle* magazines don't tell me anything actually new. After all, the bikes they describe are about fifty years old, and I knew those bikes when they were new. But there's still something interesting in each one. I love the old ads where everything sells for pennies compared to today. Many of the pictures of road tests and races are new to me, and the writers are great even if I've read their stories before. So I hope that your reading and rereading of the Bible also brings together old and new. Make new combinations between the seven themes and see new connections between the Bible's people and events. The words are always wonderful. They're fresh and never musty. And you won't need to air out your Bible in the garage before you start reading.

LET'S START AT A NEW BEGINNING

Perhaps the best place to begin is with our own new beginning. Noah is the new start for the world, and with Noah we can see three of our themes at work. Noah fulfills the themes of "It's Not the First but the Second That Counts" and also "One Stands in Place of Us All." Certainly, Noah (the second) is the new Adam (the first) by which all the world traces its line, illustrating the first/second theme. Also, the first image of the frightening sky of Noah's flood is not what lasts. The image that counts is the second one: the lasting promise of mercy in the rainbow. Patiently, Noah built the ark for decades with only the aid of his small family so that the world might continue after the flood, illustrating the "One Stands in Place of Us All" theme.

But besides the first/second and "One Stands in Place of Us All" themes in Noah, he also shows two dimensions of the "What Does Greatness Look Like?" theme. When he began to build the ark, how foolish it must have appeared. People must have mocked him daily. There was nothing grand in his first years of building. But when the flood came and that astonishing ark, 450 feet long, began to float safely, everyone could see its greatness. The ark endured over a year as the home for Noah and his family. What a sturdy majesty it had, finally ending on the mountain peak. So

Noah shows both dimensions of the greatness theme, blending together with "One Stands in Place of Us All" and "It's Not the First but the Second That Counts."

Another combination of first/second and greatness themes comes with Elisha and the Syrian army. Remember that the Syrian army surrounded Elisha's city one night, intent on killing Elisha and his servant. Elisha, however, assured his frightened servant, "Do not be afraid, for those who are with us are more than those who are with them" (2 Kings 6:16). He then prayed that God would open the servant's eyes, and "behold, the mountain was full of horses and chariots of fire all around Elisha" (2 Kings 6:17). What a combination of these themes. At first, we see only the Syrian army, and they seem the embodiment of power and greatness. But then we see the second army of angels, horses, and chariots of fire. The second army is greater than the first, and this angel army certainly looks as we expect divine greatness to look. We might also see our theme of "Instant Perfection—Patient Relationship" at work. The servant was invited to have faith in God's patient relationship and care, though that faith was certainly bolstered when, in an instant, he could see the perfection of the heavenly army.

FAMILIES, FAMILIES, CAN'T WE ALL GET ALONG?

Picture camping, especially in tents in the rain. Or think of an overcrowded Thanksgiving dinner with all the family. What do these have in common? They both look like a good idea from a distance but a bit harder to endure when they actually happen. Like our "Instant Perfection—Patient Relationship" theme, camping and having the whole family over looks perfect when you first suggest it, but both require real patience within the relationship when the rain comes or when the two dogs start fighting in the living room. So we have some of this same theme with the ending of the parable of the prodigal son in Luke 15. When the younger son returns, the father instantly celebrates with an elaborate and costly party. The younger son receives a welcome of instant perfection, which embitters the older brother. His complaint to his father, however, expresses the theme of patient relationship, though he considers that time and relationship as nothing. The son complains, "Look, these many years I have served you, and I never disobeyed your command" (Luke 15:29). But the father emphasizes this time together, saying, "Son, you are always with me, and all that is mine is yours" (Luke 15:31). The younger son came home, not for the instant celebration but for the patient relationship, which his older brother disregarded.

We might also see an interesting use of the first/second theme in the parable. The older brother would likely argue that it is just like his younger brother to be more important to his father. The firstborn stayed home and worked but got no special attention, but the second son squandered the family's money and got all the attention. But we might also see that the parable is an unusual change from the pattern of the two previous parables, the lost sheep and the lost coin. In those, the shepherd and the woman both immediately leave all to search for the lost sheep and coin. But when the younger brother leaves, the father stays with his older son. The younger son returns, and only then does the father leave to search for a lost son, the older son. It is not the first son who returns who makes the celebration complete, but it is the second son, the older son, who must be sought and who must come back to complete the party.

We aren't told exactly the arguments the brothers likely had before the prodigal son left home. But with another biblical family, we know quite well what anger led to another son going far from home. Joseph dreamed that he would rule over his brothers and further irritated them by wearing the many-colored coat that their father, Jacob, gave him as a sign of his favoritism (Genesis 37:1–11). The

> It is not the first son who returns who makes the celebration complete.

dreams of being the sheaf of grain that loomed over all others and being the one to whom sun, moon, and stars bowed down were certainly examples of greatness looking like greatness. But that was a greatness that the brothers couldn't stand, so they threw Joseph into the pit and later sold him into slavery. As the caravan bearing him off to Egyptian slavery left, the brothers likely asked, "Where are your dreams now?" The outward greatness of ruling would be hidden for years, and only a sturdy faith would define Joseph's greatness.

In Joseph, we see not only the two sides of greatness at work but also the theme of illness becoming the cure. Dreams were the problem that left him a slave in Egypt. If only he hadn't dreamt of greatness, and if only he had kept the dreams to himself, none of this would have happened. So we would tell him, "Joseph, have nothing to do with dreams! They're only trouble for you." But of course, dreams became the cure. After Joseph was imprisoned, the dreams of the baker, cupbearer, and eventually Pharaoh delivered Joseph out of prison and to the throne, where he experienced the outward greatness that he had foreseen.

IT'S ALL IN YOUR PERSPECTIVE

One of the reasons I love reading the old *Cycle* magazines is to remind myself of how much work old motorcycles were. You started them by setting the choke on the carburetor just right, cracking open the throttle just enough, and then kicking, often many, many times. Depending on the bike, prayer was the most important step. Now my modern bikes are all fuel injected and, of course, electric start. Turn the key, push the button, and they're running. Read fifty-year-old *Cycle* magazines while sitting in a hundred-year-old Model T Ford, and you'll really appreciate modern engines.

So also reading about Joseph's family puts your own in a much better light. No matter what challenges you're facing, that family likely had far more. After all, you didn't sell your brother into slavery out of a pit, did you? But a family turned upside down can be the very place where God does His work. For example, in Luke 1 we find a family upended by a shocking gift. The themes of "Grace Upends Our World" and "What Does Greatness Look Like?" intertwine for Zechariah. At the beginning of Luke, Zechariah the priest was offering the prayers when the angel Gabriel told him the gracious news that he and his wife, Elizabeth, would finally have a child. Instead of reacting with joy or even godly caution, Zechariah questioned Gabriel as to how this could be, given his age. Gabriel answered, certainly with an appearance and voice that defined greatness as greatness. "I am Gabriel. I stand in the presence of God, and I was sent to speak to you and to bring you this good news. And behold, you will be silent and unable to speak until the day that these things take place, because you did not believe my words" (Luke 1:19–20). The grace of this coming child certainly upended Zechariah's world as he became mute for nine months.

However, this grace that brought silence was also a grace that opened up a lasting song. Upon naming his son John on the eighth day, suddenly Zechariah could speak. Then he spoke of the greatness to come in his son's life: "And you, child, will be called the prophet of the Most High; for you will go before the Lord to prepare His ways, to give knowledge of salvation to His people in the forgiveness of their sins" (Luke 1:76–77). Here is a greatness that comes with the power and fanfare we expect. John fulfills that side of our greatness theme as he baptizes in the Jordan. Mark 1:5 defines that glory by the number of people going to see him: "And all the country of Judea and all Jerusalem were going out to him and were being baptized by him in the river Jordan." In Zechariah's waiting and in the coming ministry of John, we see grace upending the world and a clear demonstration of greatness.

The other side of greatness, along with the theme of patient relationship, comes soon after the birth of John the Baptist. In

Luke 2:22–32, Jesus, eight days old, is presented at the temple. His coming fulfills the long-held hope of Simeon, to whom it had been revealed that he would not die without seeing the Lord's Christ (Luke 2:26). We don't know Simeon's age, but we can surmise that he was very advanced in years. What an example of patient relationship he was. He is joined in this patient waiting by Anna, the aged widow in the temple. She also took up the infant Jesus that day and gave thanks for His arrival.

Besides the decades of patient waiting in their relationship with God, Anna and Simeon were also able to recognize the hidden greatness of the infant Jesus as the Messiah. There was no outward majesty for them to see. Here was only an infant, recently moved from the stable and manger. His parents held no titles and were called no noble names. He was unnoticed by everyone else. But Simeon, led by the Spirit, recognized Him. Simeon spoke of this glory, saying, "For my eyes have seen Your salvation that You have prepared in the presence of all peoples, a light for revelation to the Gentiles, and for glory to Your people Israel" (Luke 2:30–32). What surprising words these must have been for others who saw Him. Likely many said, "I just don't see it." But for Simeon and Anna, here was the ideal combination of a sudden, perfect display of greatness for which they had waited decades.

WHAT IS WAITING TO BE SEEN?

It's a perfect morning as I write this. The sun is rising up over Lake Michigan, and the few light clouds are sliding east across a pale blue sky. No wind, not too cold. I should stop writing and go for a ride. Take a motorcycle and see what's on the road. But, you could ask, what's left to see on roads I've seen a thousand times? I don't know, but I won't have seen those roads in exactly this light, and I won't see what's there if I stay here. I've got to get on the road. (By the way, pause here for a moment. I really am going for a motorcycle ride right now. Be back soon.)

Back now. When I was on the road, I looked east to see the sun splashing a streak of light on Lake Michigan. Turned west for home and watched the roofs sparkle from the frost. For a December morning in Wisconsin, it was a perfect morning ride.

No matter whether you've just come off the road or are sitting at home, I hope that you have that same feeling as you look at your well-worn Bible. You've turned the corners from Matthew to Mark, from Galatians to Ephesians so often there's a trail worn between them. What's there to see anymore? I don't know, but I do know two things. You've never seen those words in the light of today, and you'll never see what's new if you don't take the trip.

So go down that same road again. Turn the corner from Philippians to Colossians and say to yourself, "I wonder what I'll see today." Maybe it will be one of the same themes again; maybe it'll be something altogether new. You've never seen it like you'll see it today, and you'll never know unless you take the trip.

I'm Not the Only One

You have to understand. I'm not the only one in our house who has old books or magazines around. Now, I'm the worst collector, that's true. My motto for old motorcycle magazines is this: buy cheap, sell never. But Holly also has a bit of a collection of her own. There are cookbooks in abundance, both old and new. She's a wonderful cook, and all of us are glad of it. So she's frequently trying out new recipes, and that can be fine. But I would point out that usually the best is already here. Her caramel apple cake is the best cake in the world. It's an apple cake made from just-picked Cortland apples, walnuts, and made-from-scratch caramel topping. Serve it warm, maybe with vanilla ice cream on the side. I dare any other cake to even show up. Her apple cake is basically a caramel apple topped by walnuts with just enough flour added to disguise it as cake. Make other recipes to prove my point if you want, but caramel apple cake is the best ever.

That's how we might see the final example of several themes coming from one small text. The Christmas story of Luke 2 is that best and final piece. While we will find several themes at work on Good Friday and Easter, the best recipe for blending the flavors of several themes at once is Luke 2.

Before we begin, what themes come to mind for you? Let me suggest several simply by recounting the chief people and actions. What themes are in a stable and a manger, and what themes are present when the heavens are opened by a choir of angels? What comes to mind when humble shepherds under a quiet night sky are then frightened to the farthest extent imaginable? The angels sing, the shepherds rush in, and yet we find a sleeping infant and Mary pondering all these things. What themes blend their colors and flavors in all that?

Your list is likely more creative than mine, but here are the themes that come to my mind: "Instant Perfection—Patient Relationship"; "What Does Greatness Look Like?"; "God Cures with the Illness Itself"; and "Perfection Welcomes Failure." Let's take the Luke 2 text and hold up each theme as they go by.

Mary and Joseph were directed to Bethlehem by Caesar Augustus for the census. Here was a ruler who could order the entire world to move, be counted, and be taxed. That was one image of greatness, but we who have eyes to see recognize that by this God was moving Mary and Joseph to Bethlehem so that Jesus would be born in the city of David, fulfilling the prophecy of Micah 5:2 and showing a humble greatness that Caesar couldn't imagine. God used the illness of taxation and moving as the cure to place the family in the right place and time. When they arrived, there was no room for them. Surely Mary hoped to deliver her child at least in a house. But there was none. Yet the illness again became the cure as the stable and manger became the eternal images of

God's grace and humility. I wonder if Joseph said to Mary when the stable was all they could have, "I'm sorry, dear, this is all we'll have." I would like to think Mary said with kindness and insight, "That's all right. It's fine. I think this is where we should be."

And so the baby was born, but that is only the beginning of the Luke 2 story. Now bring on the angels and the shepherds. Let the glory of the Lord shine all around these men and turn up their terror to the highest setting. Here was greatness looking like greatness! The angel's message gives us the perfect blend of greatness in both flavors—humility and open power: "For unto you is born this day in the city of David a Savior, who is Christ the Lord. And this will be a sign for you; you will find a baby wrapped in swaddling cloths and lying in a manger" (Luke 2:11–12). Here is David's Son and the Savior of the world. And if all the greatness and glory of the chorus of angels is not enough for you, then here is your sign: not more angels, not more glimpses into heaven's court. No, a baby lying in a manger. God's ultimate glory born in a stable.

And so they went. Shepherds were not usually welcomed into towns, especially at night. But these humble, surprised men were the ones gathered around Mary, Joseph, and Jesus that night. His perfection drew them and welcomed them. Rather than seeing these men as intruders, Mary listened to all they said, and then "Mary treasured up all these things, pondering them in her heart" (Luke 2:19). No gifts could they bring, only the words given them by the angel. But that was the perfect gift.

It's that combination of perfection and patience that sums up Christmas Eve best. Jesus is perfect and comes, if not in an instant for Mary, then certainly with unexpected haste for the shepherds. When they found Him, they saw He was perfect since He was the Savior. But His coming was the first day of the long, patient relationship Mary and Joseph would have with Him and the

No gifts could they bring, only the words given them by the angel.

relationship that He extends to us all. Imagine Mary that night, after the shepherds have left, holding her Son and wondering about all that might come. How she might have talked with Him, asked Him what He would do, and asked what she should do? How to be the mother of the Savior of the world? What a wonderful, lasting relationship of patience and love began that night.

A perfect recipe needs only a few strong ingredients that match well. Apples, walnuts, caramel, and flour are the heart of great cake. So two-sided greatness, welcoming perfection, illness becoming the cure, and an instant perfection that stretches into a lifelong patient relationship—these four themes make Christmas Eve the best time to see our themes blending together.

> What a wonderful, lasting relationship of patience and love began that night.

Now It's Your Recipe

Following someone else's recipe is fine, safe, and repeatable. But sometimes you want to make your own. Now it's your turn to make your own biblical theme. I suspect that you've been doing that all along. You've noticed repeated patterns of action, seen returns to a particular place or situation, and found people met in the same ways by God. Likely also, you've expected one of my themes to be said a bit differently from the way I have it here. With all that, you're ready to suggest your own biblical themes.

If you've already done this, I would love to meet you and hear your ideas. I'm sure that right now you have that eager look that students have in class, the look that says, "Call on me, call on me. I'm ready." I'm also sure that your ideas surpass the seven themes I have here. Continue to build on those ideas, trying out different biblical texts to see how your themes work in them.

However, if you're not sure of possible biblical themes, I'll suggest two ideas that might work for you. One is a single verse that applies to many biblical suggestions, and the other is an often-repeated event that begs to be summarized in a theme. The first is the single verse Psalm 30:5: "For His anger is but for a moment, and His favor is for a lifetime. Weeping may tarry for the night, but joy comes with the morning." Here is another two-part theme with a sharp contrast between them. We know these opposites of weeping and joy so well. The night of weeping stretches our patience. Nothing goes slower than a long night of worry, pain, or loneliness. Time stops, but our mind is racing with worry. But this verse promises that a joyful morning is coming. Yes, we may someday understand or appreciate why we experienced a troubled night. But more important, actual joy will come. What a wonderful promise made by David and, better, made by God Himself to everyone who reads and believes. How you might phrase or title this, I'll leave to you. You might use simply the words of the verse, or you might have a distinctive summary of your own.

The other possible theme involves a situation that is repeated many times over in the Bible. The barren woman has a child. Think of the examples, both the famous ones and those lesser known. Sarah and Abraham had their only son, Isaac, when Sarah was ninety. Then we have other Old Testament examples such as Hannah, the mother of Samuel, who prayed earnestly for a child (1 Samuel 1). Also there is the birth of a child to the Shunammite woman who befriended Elisha and was granted a son. She then lost her son to a sudden illness, but Elisha raised him up from the dead (2 Kings 4). These women prepare us for the births of John to the elderly Elizabeth and the birth of Jesus to Mary. What summarizes these important births? How would you capture these women's time of waiting, waiting sometimes in patience, sometimes in resignation? What does the gift of a child say about the creative power of God, His love of expressing Himself through His own creation, and His purposeful plan for these so unlikely born children? I'll leave it to you to formulate the exact name and phrasing of this theme, but these births deserve to be recognized.

Perfection and Patience One More Time

Throughout this book, we've discussed perfection and patience repeatedly, both as a first theme and as a tension through all the following themes. Even here, in formulating your own biblical themes, perfection and patience are at work. You know there's a biblical pattern waiting to be seen, even more than just the two I suggested just now. But if the exact words don't come for you right away, be patient. The perfect pattern isn't going anywhere. It's not like buying old *Cycle* magazines. I have two issues that I'm still missing: July 1968 and April 1970. If I see them, maybe I should jump on them and buy them, even if they're more than the usual $5 each. After all, you can't buy happiness, but you can buy old *Cycle* magazines. And think, maybe that one issue that's for sale is the only one left in the world. If I don't get it, it could be gone for good. Holly, however, really doubts that there is anyone besides me who actually wants these old magazines. So maybe I can wait on it and let the price come down.

But you don't have that worry. The biblical text isn't going to be sold out from under you. It's unlikely you're going to find someone else has worked out your theme before you do. So be patient with divine perfection. You'll have time to fill out the examples and define the action and its importance. The right words and understanding will come. In fact, praying about that would be a wonderful example of a patient relationship that waits for His perfect insight.

I trust that the interaction of those two, perfection and patience, have been expressed in various ways with each theme. We want instant and lasting perfection. But God's timing stresses patience above all. His perfection so often uses the very opposite of what we expect. So don't be dismayed when the first is not everything you hope for. Be patient, another is coming. Don't be caught up in the many people and the worries each one brings in your life. Don't despair as the problems multiply faster than God's answers. He loves to answer all with one solution. He thrives on standing alone, one in place of us all.

When God has taken this single, solitary place for our sake, your life will never be the same. His grace comes to upend your world. However, it might not bring the instant perfection that you expect. Trust that He has indeed stood in your place, and trust Him when your world appears upended. Remember the heroes of faith who were called by grace to follow His path for them— Mary, Peter, Gideon, Esther, and Paul. They stepped out on a long walk in their relationship with God while grace spun their world around.

On that grace-led walk, we expect a perfect, instant greatness that at least we can recognize. It would be nice if the rest of the world could recognize it too. That might come with all the suddenness of an angel chorus breaking open heaven on Christmas Eve night. But be patient. Greatness often comes in hidden ways. It might take time and patience to recognize God at work and to see more than just a baby lying in a manger.

But doesn't anyone see the problem here? A baby left to be born in a stable, lying in a manger? Are you angels just going to watch this? Are you shepherds just going to leave Him there? Isn't anyone going to fix this? Amidst worry and impatience, we need to remember that with God, the illness is often the cure. The fix is already here. The problem is solved in the problem itself. We don't have to get busy and find Him the perfect room. He's in that perfect room already—the stable and the manger are what He always wanted. If you want a cure for impatience, here's the theme for you. The illness is the cure itself.

That draws us toward Him in wonder. That's really the only way we can approach God and have a patient relationship with Him. His instant perfection ought to always drive us away, frightened and thankful that we escaped with our small, dark lives. But God welcomes our failures, and strangely we're drawn toward

Him, even when His greatness is on display. But He draws us not merely to dazzle or destroy us. He brings us to Himself for love and life. God so loves us that He must share His life with us, so He brings us within His perfection through His Son. Perfection and patience come together as He welcomes the failures that we are.

That's the wonder of these themes and the Word of God. It is God's message for all and yet also His message for each of us. Sitting next to my computer is a copy of *Cycle* magazine that has a test on my first new motorcycle, a Yamaha CT-1 175 Enduro. To you, it's just an old magazine, but to me, it's a trip back almost fifty years ago. The editors loved the bike, and come to think of it, it was a great bike. I wouldn't mind finding one again. But the Word of God is better than this. It is the timeless message of God's mercy over each of us. It is His past, present, and future view of us as His beloved children. That message never grows old, never changes, and draws us to itself every day.

I trust that you will continue to work with these two key ideas of patience and perfection. You'll continue to see new repeated actions and key ideas throughout the Scriptures and will also re-organize our list here with your own new pieces. Perhaps no list will ever be perfect since now we see in a mirror dimly. But that's all right, because God in His patience is pleased when we read and think about what He's done, again and again. He is perfectly patient with us. Look for the landmarks of His repeated actions, be comforted by what you expect, and rejoice in what is new again in today's travel. God bless your reading of His Word as a journey, both familiar and new.

"WHAT A FRIEND WE HAVE IN JESUS"

It's hard to have one final hymn, one hymn to capture all our themes and the new ones you're creating. But for patience and perfection, it's hard to do better than "What a Friend We Have in Jesus" (*LSB* 770). It begins with a contrast between our own attempts to carry our worries and the One who alone can bear them. One stands in place of us all when we bring those worries to Him alone.

> What a friend we have in Jesus,
>> All our sins and griefs to bear!
> What a privilege to carry
>> Ev'rything to God in prayer!
> Oh, what peace we often forfeit;
>> Oh, what needless pain we bear—
> All because we do not carry
>> Ev'rything to God in prayer!

It wonderfully expresses the theme of having a patient relationship with God in stanza 2: "Can we find a friend so faithful Who will all our sorrows share? Jesus knows our every weakness—Take it to the Lord in prayer." It also pictures the welcome we receive in His perfection, even when all we bring are our worries. The beginning of stanza 3 says, "Are we weak and heavy laden, Cumbered with a load of care? Precious Savior, still our refuge—Take it to the Lord in prayer." So often we turn first to our friends and our own solutions and only as a second step do we pray. The hymn ends with that contrast in stanza 3: "Do thy friends despise, forsake thee? Take it to the Lord in prayer. In His arms He'll take and shield thee; Thou wilt find a solace there."

While other hymns might capture these hopes, this hymn pictures us in a lasting relationship of prayer. His answers are promised, but we don't need to see them yet. For now, the perfection is His welcome and His listening. The perfection we seek is the Friend that He already is.

Discussion Questions

1. The chapter started with my finding old motorcycle magazines to read. What old favorite books or magazines do you reread, or what movies and TV shows do you watch over and over? What is the attraction of going back to these familiar stories?

2. We may know the Bible's story very well, and yet we read it again and again. To which Bible books do you often return? When especially do you go to that book or that chapter?

3. When you reread a particular Bible text, are you looking for something new, an insight that's escaped you, or are you reading for reassurance and a change in emotion?

4. The chapter combined several themes with certain Bible events. Which of the seven themes can you see working in the following texts and events?

    *   Jesus and the disciples sharing the Last Supper and Jesus' Words of Institution of the Supper (Matthew 26:26–29)

- Jesus and the two thieves on the cross, especially the repentant thief (Luke 23:39–43)

- Jesus' appearance with the two men walking on the Emmaus Road (Luke 24:13–35)

5. On the other hand, what two or three themes have you seen working together in a particular text? For example, you might see the first/second theme and "What Does Greatness Look Like?" in several places and sequences of people and events.

6. I encouraged you to develop your own themes and suggested two in this chapter: the night/morning—weeping/joy image of Psalm 30:5 and the birth of a child to the barren woman. How would you express the essential truth of these two ideas?

7. Finally, you might have noticed patterns of repeated action that I haven't noticed or mentioned. What themes of your own have come up in your reading? Remember that if you haven't seen any yet, be patient as His perfect Word will always be there, waiting for you to see more tomorrow.